A CONDITIONAL EMBRACE

BLACK PERFORMANCE AND CULTURAL CRITICISM
E. Patrick Johnson, Series Editor

A CONDITIONAL EMBRACE

BLACK QUEER FEMINISM IN PERFORMANCE

Kristyl D. Tift

THE OHIO STATE UNIVERSITY PRESS
COLUMBUS

Library of Congress Cataloging-in-Publication Data

Names: Tift, Kristyl Dawn, author

Title: A conditional embrace : Black queer feminism in performance / Kristyl D. Tift.

Other titles: Black performance and cultural criticism

Description: Columbus : The Ohio State University Press, [2026] | Series: Black performance and cultural criticism | Includes bibliographical references and index. | Summary: "Analyzes the contributions of twentieth- and twenty-first-century theater and film artists Shirlene Holmes, Sharon Bridgforth, Staceyann Chin, Donnetta Lavinia Grays, and Dee Rees, exploring how these artists represent Black queer women's survival through processes of self-making, community-building, and homemaking"—Provided by publisher.

Identifiers: LCCN 2026012260 | ISBN 9780814216194 hardback | ISBN 0814216196 hardback | ISBN 9780814285039 ebook | ISBN 0814285031 ebook

Subjects: LCSH: American drama—African American authors—20th century—History and criticism | American drama—African American authors—21st century—History and criticism | Drama—Black authors—21st century—History and criticism | African American women dramatists—Southern States—20th century | African American women dramatists—Southern States—21st century | African Americans in the performing arts—Caribbean Area | African American theater—History—20th century | African American theater—History—21st century | African American women in motion pictures | Women, Black—In motion pictures | Motion pictures—History—20th century | Motion pictures—History—21st century | African American lesbians—Southern States—Social conditions | Lesbians, Black—Caribbean Area—Social conditions | Queer theory | Feminist theater

Classification: LCC PS338.B53 T54 2026

LC record available at https://lccn.loc.gov/2026012260

Other identifiers: ISBN 9780814259900 (paperback) | ISBN 0814259901 (paperback)

Cover design by Ashley Muehlbauer
Text design by Juliet Williams
Type set in Adobe Minion Pro

♾ The paper used in this publication meets the minimum requirements of the American National Standard for Information Sciences—Permanence of Paper for Printed Library Materials. ANSI Z39.48-1992.

To Lauryn Elise, who is like my own. I love you deeply.

CONTENTS

ILLUSTRATIONS

INTRODUCTION

Storms

Critical inquiries into Southern Black queer pasts are often sticky, with the project of Black queer futurity taking a back seat to excavations of gaps and erasures in history. While gazing back to the past for historiographical purposes can propel societies forward, there is a material risk to the present being overlooked in its favor. In *A Dirty South Manifesto,* L. H. Stallings opens by comparing the regulatory conditions of the "Old" South and the "New" South, acknowledging that regional politics of the past and the present are undeniably linked. Stallings observes: "While persons living in southern states typically classified under the broad rubric 'the South' know that there is not one South but many, there are historical narratives that have ignored the development of multiple Souths."[1] Stallings, here, recognizes that contemporary acts and embodiments and their social significances are often stuck (or suspended) in time, until later, when a historian recovers it; that is, if an archive or a living griot exists. For marginalized people, the archive may never be recorded and later may never come. It is crucial, therefore, to reconsider what constitutes a reliable archive for underacknowledged histories to emerge. This book, *A Conditional Embrace: Black Queer Feminism in Performance,* is a thoughtful recovery effort in which documented and living histories are excavated for critical ends.

1. Stallings, *Dirty South Manifesto,* 2.

My approach to reading the past into the present is guided by Diana Taylor's vision of what an archive can be. Exploring diverse embodied performances of the Southern Hemisphere, Taylor's *The Archive and the Repertoire* reassesses "performative artifacts" of the not-so-distant past—performances, which, in their time, and to outsiders looking in, may have seemed inconsequential but are, in fact, embodied social and cultural knowledge deserving of preservation and production. Cookie Woolner's *The Famous Lady Lovers,* an interesting historical survey of Black queer women living, loving, and performing in public before the Stonewall Riots, exemplifies how an array of seemingly disparate artifacts, when considered intertextually, can evince an archive that reinstitutes Black queer women performers in the historical record. Situating her study in an era before queer, feminist, and Black Power movements were popular, Woolner proves that the absence of Black queer herstories in theater and performance research presents an opportunity to recover those stories and rediscover their tellers. Woolner recognizes the significance of the theater as a space in which women like Ethel Waters, Gladys Bentley, and Bessie Smith publicly revealed, albeit indirectly, their sexual identities in performance during repressive times.[2] Northern Black queer women are the primary foci of Woolner's study as Northern spaces have, historically, been more tolerant (and, at times, welcoming) of the presence and performances of Black queer people. The performative artifacts of Black queer women in the more conservative Southern US, however, are often unrecorded, lost, or encoded.

Leaning on archives of old and new, traditional and nontraditional, written and oral, *A Conditional Embrace: Black Queer Feminism in Performance* attempts to decode the dramatic narratives and visual dramas of Black women theater and performance artists creating in a Black queer feminist aesthetic with a Southern sensibility and love ethic. This book assesses the role of race, gender, and sexuality in Black women's lives as animated in historical and contemporary performance, broadly defined. My analysis of selected theater, film, and literary works written between the late twentieth and early twenty-first centuries reflects an attempt to fill in some "Black w(h)oles" in Black *and* queer performance history, theory, and criticism.[3] While the US South and the Caribbean are sites of investigation in this book, it was not my intent to write a book about "Southern" Black queer women artists. When I began this research, I sought to unearth Black plays with central or marginal characters who were unapologetically queer in their sexuality and/or gender

2. See Woolner, *Famous Lady Lovers.*
3. See Hammonds, "Black (W)holes."

presentation. Recovering one playwright whose work spoke to this intent led to another which led to another, and as I continued to dig, I found that the artists and their narratives had roots in the US South or the Global South.

While a Southern perspective adds flavor and richness, it also enhances conflict. The regional politics of respectability across lines of race, color, sexuality, and religion often threaten the livelihoods and comfort of Black queer people. In Donnetta Lavinia Grays's solo play *the cowboy is dying,* for example, an eight-year-old Donnetta "wrestles" with God in the backyard of her parents' South Carolina home. It is hurricane season and a storm is coming. The storm may seem unimportant—hurricanes, tornadoes, and tropical storms regularly threaten communities in the Southern United States and the Caribbean—however, it is a metaphor for a storm whirling inside her with respect to her developing sexual identity and the familial and communal resistance she will experience because of it. No matter the extent of their impact, all storms have consequences, the emotional, psychophysical, and material toll of which may vary. And for the survivors, there is a cultural understanding that another storm is always on the horizon.

Similarly, in Southern literature, hurricanes serve as plot devices which often determine the characters' fates. Harlem Renaissance writer and anthropologist Zora Neale Hurston vividly documents the impact of one such hurricane in her 1937 novel *Their Eyes Were Watching God.* The classic story focuses on Janie, a Black female heroine living in Eatonville, Florida. Janie enters the story as a carefree teenage girl who, unbeknown to her, will soon be forced into marriage with an older man, Logan Killicks, at her grandmother's behest. Only later in life, when Janie is well into her forties and after two loveless marriages, does she explore her romantic and sexual desires on her own terms through a love affair with Teacake. Hurston's story not only centers on a woman's desire but presents Black women's romantic autonomy and individualism with rare candor for its time. But as quickly as Janie finds love, it is taken from her by the hurricane, leaving her transformed for better and for worse.

Storms can do that; they can change you. When they make landfall, they disrupt, reconfigure worlds, and leave survivors to collect the pieces of their pasts to forge reimagined futures. Some storms cause divisions in familial units, displacing one from another and obliterating kinships. Little Donnetta's connection with God and her traditional family unit is threatened by an internal storm representing the tug-of-war with oneself that often arises when coming out as a lesbian in the Black South. The Black queer feminist narratives of Donnetta Lavinia Grays, Dee Rees, Sharon Bridgforth, Shirlene Holmes, and Staceyann Chin provide a kaleidoscope of interconnected subjectivities which harken to past performances of Black queer womanhood while nodding to those of the future. Navigating metaphorical and figurative storms, their characters' quotidian existences are inevitably disturbed, necessitating the deconstruction of normative ideas of race, gender, and sexuality imposed upon them. To not only survive but thrive in Black Southern spaces, they encounter the storms of racism, sexism, and homophobia; rebuild themselves in their own image; haul off the storm's rubble; and redesign home and community for that reconfigured self. And, commonly, they do this in partnership with other Black queer folk, in what I call acts of *lovin' on*—a concept inspired by a humorous yet subversive *teachable moment* I experienced as a student.

Put Your Lovin' On Me

One summer while in graduate school at the University of Georgia, my close friend, Angela, and I took a seminar on women, biology, and reproduction. During a class discussion about "the affective turn," our professor—whom we genuinely respected—openly questioned feminist scholars' turn to love. A progressive white feminist who also taught queer theory courses, she sat perplexed by the shift in focus from feminist radical resistance to misogyny and heterocentrism characteristic of second-wave feminism to this "sudden" turn to explorations of love as resistance. She declared with much flair, "F*ck love!" Instinctively, Angela and I laughed. Then, realizing our professor was quite serious, we looked at each other bemused then back to her with disciplined curiosity. We wanted her to unpack her disdain for love, but she did not. I don't believe she could articulate her frustration in that moment, as she seemed to be working through it in real time, but she had a visceral response to the idea that love could be an effective tool of resistance. Although Black feminist thinkers like Audre Lorde, Cheryl Clarke, and bell hooks had convincingly argued for love as resistance in their writing for decades—writings our professor knew quite well—there was still something about using love in this way that she found off-putting, weak, and ineffective to the project of dismantling the systems responsible for the "isms" of the world. As Black women, Angela and I understood the uses of love in movement-building. As *Southern* Black women, we understood how the passion of love can translate to action as evidenced by the survival of our ancestors and the reality of our very existence. When love is the only weapon you have to change your circumstances, you devise inventive ways to wield it.

That provocative moment led me to the realization that for marginalized people, especially those only a generation or two removed from the darkest eras in history, love has emancipatory possibilities, and whether we embrace it or not, human survival depends on it. In the 1970 documentary *Meeting the Man,* James Baldwin tells an audience in France, "Love has never been a popular movement. And no one's ever wanted really to be free. The world is held together, really it is, held together by the love and the passion of a very few people."[4] The profundity and simplicity of his statement reveals a solution so simple that it seems a preposterous remedy, but if Baldwin is right, and I believe he is, that love is the solution to hatred, then embodied acts of lovin' on oneself and *some*body else can defy even the most harried attempts to dispel its potency.[5]

Black love is as complex as Black politics (social, economic, or otherwise), and there is more than one way to love in Black cultural contexts. It is generally understood that people of the diaspora are not a monolith and that the love politics among them vary widely from heterosexual cisgender relationships to polyamorous communes and beyond. Considering the generational influence of conservatism on African Americans, necessitated by enforced labor and assimilation by enslavers who stole away with their bodies then forced them to work the stolen lands of Indigenous people, it could be argued that less traditional ways of lovin' on one's body or other bodies, including but not exclusively erotic lovin', do the work of combatting the mental, physical, and spatial restrictions of a racist national past and present. Historical webs of theft, deceit, violence, and control reveal the depths of Black pain and the importance and utility of radical love practices to dull that ache (like dancing in a club until the wee hours of the morning, alone and unbothered, or in somebody's arms drunk with freedom). Imagining love as a political act, Darnell L. Moore, reading bell hooks, rightly asserts that "Love, in fact, is animated through our connections, mutual understanding, and community."[6]

Lovin' on, as a critical framework, is a communal and individual effort toward connection as expressed through eroticism, storytelling, spiritual bonding or praise, platonic intimacy, and self-directed love acts. While it can be a solo act, lovin' on is most effective in covenants with one or more bodies. Spiritual lovin' on, for example, is prominent in the works of Black queer feminist performance (BQFP) artists of the South. While religion and spirituality are key themes in their works, they do not necessarily share the same function—although there are similarities in that both involve traditional practices that are repeated and repeatable. Spiritual lovin' on, as demonstrated by

4. See Dixon's short documentary, *Meeting the Man: James Baldwin in Paris.*

5. A few truths remain regarding love: (1) There is no science as to whom and how one loves; (2) There is no mathematical equation for how best to execute love; and (3) It *is.*

6. See Moore, "Black Radical Love," 326. For more on Black radical love practices and ethics of care, see Reed's *Love and Abolition* and Nneka Dennie's *Mary Ann Shadd Cary.*

the women characters at the center of these works, is often animated through ritual practices that reify their faith in themselves, their bond with another person or persons, and a greater purpose for their lives. This is most clearly exemplified in the works of Shirlene Holmes and Sharon Bridgforth, whose characters practice Christianity (most visibly outside of the home, in church) and Africanist spirituality (in the home, at an altar, or on "blessed" ground). While religion and spirituality coexist in the works, religion does not appear to transform the characters as deeply, immediately, and consistently as spirituality does.

While religion instructs their fundamental moral and ethical codes, for each central figure—even the solo artist, like Staceyann Chin and Donnetta Lavinia Grays, who are both the artist and the subject of their autobiographical works—acts of spiritual lovin' on propel them toward belief systems that best serve their visions for their Black queer futures. This reflects, in some regard, an unspoken truism in Black communities wherein folks carry religion and spirituality alongside each other in daily life. Many Black families with roots in the South incorporate spiritual practices to protect loved ones and ensure that their family remains whole, practices that cannot be found anywhere in a religious text but have been passed down through generations. Consider my Southern African Methodist Episcopalian mother's annual practice and instruction that I refrain from washing or drying clothes on New Year's Day because "you might wash someone out of the family." A trusted myth passed down through generations, this spiritual lovin' on practice, which is, in part, her way of protecting the family, has a practical function when adhered to at the appropriate time and, moreover, it meets the needs of her spirit.

In religious spaces, weekly gatherings for prayer are often held, a ritual that in its repetition is meant to create beloved communities through faith and service. However, membership in these spaces, in the South and Global South, for queer people, can be exclusive to heterosexual and straight-passing people. Acknowledging this phenomenon in Black social and civil rights movements, to which the church has historically been key, Moore continues:

> I cannot, for instance, recount the number of times some Black person whose confessed love for Black people stopped short of justice for Black trans and gender-nonconforming people. I cannot tell you how often I've come across some Black cisgender heterosexual man arguing why a specific focus on Black women and girls . . . is dangerous to movement work because of the ways it splits an imagined Black political agenda.[7]

7. Moore, "Black Radical Love," 326.

Moore observes the ways that those of us who express love for Black people and culture fall short of lovin' on the people we call our own because of differences on gender, sex, and sexuality. While Black love politics are contradictory at times, they are also deeply utopian, as the effort to love on ourselves and somebody else, as I believe Baldwin urges us to realize and actualize, is the most affordable and accessible form of activism.

Lovin' on somebody and being loved on by another body without conditions, even in traumatic times, is transformative. In Black Southern communities, to love on is to take care of something or someone regardless of relation. Signifying an act of self-love or self-care (as in, "No, I can't go. I'm lovin on' me today"), or lovin' on someone else emotionally, spiritually, financially, or sexually requires dedication to *some* body. It requires intention and connection to the body, especially when said bodies are identifiably of-color, queer, and woman. These bodies need protection, allyship, and covering—a truth which has long led to the emergence of subcultures in which marginalized folk can be themselves without the state monitoring their speech and actions. Artistic representations of Black queer women lovin' on themselves and/or somebody else counter the historical lack of visibility of such people while challenging unsteady and false notions of Blackness that disavow queerness. When dramatic and visual narratives of Black queer people lovin' are, at least, recognized and, at best, understood in majority Black spaces, the opportunity for a shared experience that transcends superficial differences reveals itself. (Love can do that.) This is clear in a variety of forms of artistic expression, including music. I am thinking, here, of the reciprocal lovin' on that inspired part 1 of Beyoncé's *Renaissance,* an album with a sonic landscape influenced by disco and house music, which the iconic singer dedicated to her beloved Uncle Jonny, a gay man who died of HIV/AIDS on July 29, 1998; she was seventeen years old. In a message on her website preceding the album's release, she wrote: "He was my godmother and the first person to expose me to a lot of the music and culture that serve as inspiration for this album. Thank you to all of the pioneers who originate culture, to all of the fallen angels whose contributions have gone unrecognized for far too long. This is a celebration for you."[8] The singer's tribute to her uncle decades after his death is a *recovery effort*—an attempt to reclaim space and time from a society and circumstance that allowed neither space nor time for such revelry.

On the 2017 album *4:44,* Beyoncé's husband, rapper Jay-Z, also engages in lovin' on as reciprocity in the song "Smile." In it, he pays tribute to his mother,

---

8. This statement was originally posted on the artist's website, http://www.beyonce.com/. It is no longer accessible there. To read it in its entirety, see Ramos, "GLAAD Honoree Beyoncé."

Gloria Carter, who came out as a lesbian that same year.[9] The rapper's lyrics reveal that she self-medicated to relieve the pressures of suppressing her sexuality and managing the sole responsibility of raising four children with little income in the drug-riddled Marcy Projects in Brooklyn in the 1970s and '80s. Integrated are a sample of Stevie Wonder's "Love's in Need of Love Today"[10] and an excerpt of his mother reading a poem about living a double life and hiding behind a false smile. "Smile" summons listeners of hip-hop—a genre of music noted for promoting themes, images, and utterances of hypermasculinity, violence, homophobia, and materialism—to hear a straight Black man openly mourn the queer woman his mother could not be while celebrating her newfound freedom. Both examples of allyship and advocacy through the acknowledgment of the value of Black queer happiness for the health of family units demonstrate that unconditional intracultural embraces across sexual identities are possible despite the fact that politics of respectability that cast out queerness are as native to Black culture, although not exclusively, as torrential storms are to the South.

"We Are a Family, Like a Giant Tree"

Acts of lovin' on are nothing new in vulnerable communities in which life and culture are always already at risk. In fact, lovin' on has often been the only way to resist attempts at domination and advance toward some semblance of freedom. I grew up in the 1980s and 1990s as the HIV/AIDS and crack cocaine epidemics ravaged the structure of Black communities. My family, too, was impacted by the latter. Back then, it was common for the crack epidemic to be discussed behind closed doors, reflecting a complicity of silence prevalent in families ashamed of their addicted relatives (a similar shame common in families with queer relatives at the time). With its numbing effects, crack—a drug capable of hijacking the body, mind, and spirit—only worsened incidents of violence, incarceration, and single- and extended-parent households. Thriving and struggling communities of color all contended with the same illicit foe because once the addiction took hold, economics did not matter. Furthermore, the US government's eventual actions to combat the crack cocaine epidemic were not specific to the communities it impacted. Instead, the "war on drugs" heralded by Richard Nixon and forwarded by Ronald Reagan—which promoted antidrug use, funded treatment programs, and passed stricter drug

9. Jay-Z, "Smile."
10. Stevie Wonder, "Love's in Need of Love."

legislation—further disadvantaged communities in need of a culturally specific, wholistic approach to healing.

HIV/AIDS was also discussed in hushed tones within and outside of the home because of its deadly impact on bisexual and gay men who were then widely considered pariahs of society. However, with the rise of intravenous drug use, HIV/AIDS began to further infiltrate Black and Brown communities, causing a national panic that resulted in the ostracization of groups of people based not only on sexuality but on race. Both epidemics converged to further disrupt the foundations of spaces whose racialized residents were all too familiar with economic instability and lack of access, resources, and political power. The proximal similarities of the impact of the HIV/AIDS and crack epidemics on families of queer and straight people is representative of Judith Butler's "up againstness"[11]—a multivalent idea of closeness that allows us to contend with the individual and collective "ethical obligations" of living within and nearby communities in crisis. Peering closely at the bodies and listening intently to the stories of the individuals at the center of both epidemics reveal a commonality: the desire for "more life."[12]

In addition to celebrities like Elizabeth Taylor, Rock Hudson, Earvin "Magic" Johnson, and Arthur Ashe, there were everyday people directly impacted by both HIV/AIDS and drug addiction, bringing awareness to both problems. In 1996 Oprah Winfrey interviewed an eleven-year-old girl named Hydeia Broadbent on her nationally syndicated talk show, *The Oprah Winfrey Show* (see figure 1). The modern face of AIDS, in the recording Broadbent appears small for her age and has a correspondingly childlike voice. Her dark hair braided thickly in a half-up, half-down style resembling a crown, Broadbent wears a small hoop nose ring and dangling rainbow-colored earrings formed in the shape of people. Tugging at the hearts of viewers in the studio and throughout the country, she speaks with a gravitas beyond her years as she explains how she contracted the virus in utero from her biological mother (who was an IV drug user). She speaks of the struggle to maintain her health as someone with a compromised immune system that leaves her susceptible to contracting other infections and diseases that might kill her. Broadbent also designates those who dehumanize people living with the virus as fearful of contracting HIV/AIDS simply by being in the same space or by touching someone infected.

---

11. Butler, "Precarious Life," 134.

12. Here, I am thinking of the earnestness in which Prior Walter, a white gay character diagnosed with AIDS in Tony Kushner's *Angels of America*, pleads to a counsel of angels for "more life" (regardless of the challenges posed by mitigated health and the deaths of lovers and friends).

FIGURE 1. Hydeia Broadbent on *The Oprah Winfrey Show*, 1996. Courtesy of Harpo, Inc.

Sitting across from one of the most recognizable journalists in the world, the little girl discusses her experience of lost innocence and isolation while expressing hope for a cure. There is a particularly poignant moment in which Winfrey plainly asks, "What's the hardest part?" to which the little girl replies, "When your friends die." Struggling to complete the thought, Broadbent is overcome by emotion as she processes the deaths of her beloved friends in real time. "They always die," she says with tears streaming down her face. Those lost friends shared her experience of spending childhood navigating a storm which, under normal conditions, during that time, usually resulted in death. The burden of advocacy work and basic survival are visible in the physicality of the petite activist: she looks tired. She looks worn down by the untenable socio-eco-political conditions which she, a little Black US American girl fighting for her life, and others living through simultaneous epidemics, had to endure. In 2024 Broadbent died at the age of thirty-nine. Surpassing expectations for her lifespan, she lived to see a world in which the virus was no longer a death sentence thanks to her and others' public testimonies and the advancements of AIDS research.[13]

---

13. Initially dubbed a "cancer" or "plague," HIV/AIDS in the 1980s and '90s was not considered the problem of *all* Americans but rather of gay Americans. Broadbent, Ryan White, and others reminded the country that no one was immune to the virus. Growing attention to HIV/AIDS led to government support and private funding for research on the progression of

In the face of fierce advocacy, HIV/AIDS—then referred to as "the gay plague" or "the gay cancer"—nearly erased an entire generation of gay men, many of whom died young and in the arms of queer nonbiological caregivers and family members. Before the US government paid attention to the virus's deleterious effect on the gay community, lesbian and bisexual women cared for those dying of the infection. Adding insult to injury, the government's delay in mitigating the spread of the virus was socially acceptable because of public homophobic sentiment. Had funding for scientific research and public health education been made available sooner, fewer gay citizens would have died. Moreover, the otherization of gay people and belief that the virus was endemic to queer folk enabled it to permeate the gay community and spill over beyond its borders into other at-risk communities.

Consensual and nonconsensual acts of pleasure-seeking, such as risky sexual behaviors and illicit drug use, can be temporary escape routes for those seeking refuge from traumatic pasts or for those in search of more pleasurable presents. The Trevor Project, which finds that "substance use is common among LGBTQ youth," states, "Regular substance use was reported more among LGBTQ youth who had experienced efforts to change their sexual orientation and/or gender identity, and among those who had experienced physical harm due to their LGBTQ identity."[14] Rejection by family members within homes of origin can lead queer youth toward acts of pleasure-seeking that have the potential to make them feel safe and loved while having adverse effects on their mental and physical health. It is not unheard of, even today, for a family to put a queer child out of the home for not conforming to gender and sexual norms. It is also not uncommon for gay and lesbian surrogate kindred to intervene and stand in the gap for at-risk youth, as exemplified in the television series *Pose* (2018–21). An homage to gay men and transwomen of color in New York City in the 1980s and '90s, season 1 follows several young queer people searching for acceptance in the "houses" of ballroom culture. The older queer heads of household (affectionately called "mother" or "father") prove invaluable in helping their "children" navigate a world in which HIV/AIDS, substance abuse, poverty, and antigay and transphobic violence are immediate mortal threats.

It is notable that becoming "family" or being "in the family" does not require a biological connection in either queer or Black communities. During American slavery, enslaved Black people were regularly separated and sold off of plantations and forced to rebuild familial units with no guarantee that the "new" family would remain intact. After emancipation (in 1863) and

---

the disease and its cure. There is still no cure, but today prophylactics such as PrEP reduce the viral load of the carrier and the risk of contracting HIV/AIDS.

14. See the Trevor Project, "Substance Use and Suicide Risk."

"Juneteenth" (June 19, 1865), formerly enslaved people searched nationwide for biological loved ones who had been sold away. As exemplified in Solomon Northup's memoir *Twelve Years a Slave,* in which Northup, a New York–born free man, is kidnapped and made to labor on a Louisiana plantation, familial separations through the sale of human chattel made reunification nearly impossible. With the devastating historical trauma of slavery as its foundation, the project of the Black US American family is still a work in progress. Compounded by succeeding social storms in the centuries since, the accumulation of traumatic excesses continues to shape the concept of family for Black *and* queer folk. The very notion of family, consequently, has been suspended in such a way that necessitates processes of reconfiguration.

Self-definition, for example, offers people living on the margins of society a chance to remake themselves by calling themselves by their own names and developing meaning and community around those names. In 1977 the Combahee River Collective wrote: "This focusing upon our own [racial-sexual] oppression is embodied in the concept of identity politics. We believe that the most profound and potentially the most radical politics come directly out of our own identity, as opposed to working to end somebody else's oppression."[15] For Black women, a group that has been empowered by self-naming, self-defining, and other embodied acts of agency and service (like public protests, sit-ins, boycotts, and performances), identity politics have served a significant purpose, enabling them to make sense of themselves in societies that tolerate them but do not celebrate them. Thus, attending to one's identity by *playing with* identifiers that feel right is an act of self-preservation that allows one to recast oneself in a materiality that sustains them. As the unhoused queer youth in *Pose* discover, there is little freedom in disregarding race, sexuality, or gender when society's treatment of them centers on those factors. In fact, their lives truly begin to take shape when they claim power by naming themselves for themselves in the arms and houses of chosen families.

Black Queer Feminist Performance

At the core of Black queer feminist performance are the principles that inform Black feminist and womanist drama aesthetics, of which Freda Scott Giles, Lisa M. Anderson, and Lynette Goddard have persuasively written. In "Methexis vs. Mimesis," Giles writes: "The Womanist dramatist mines the experiences of her foremothers, and her own experiences, passed through history, myth,

15. Guy-Sheftall, *Words of Fire,* 239.

culture, symbols, dreams, and inspiration, for the creation of the dramatic event."[16] Similarly, Anderson observes that Black feminist playwrights "incorporate history into their works, ensuring that the histories they tell reveal an otherwise hidden history" in addition to "fully embrac[ing] the questions of representation of black women" while "work[ing] to refine and reshape them."[17] Goddard, like Giles, asserts that Black feminist performance "is distinctly political" and "endeavor[s] to explore the limits of oppression and the ways that Black women are positioned by racist, (hetero)sexist discourses."[18] Challenging the status quo, theater artists and filmmakers working in a Black queer feminist aesthetic position Black queer women within intersectional, intertemporal, and interspatial narrative contexts which are consistently, but not exclusively, woman-centric.

The existence of homophobia in Black communities cannot be ignored in these works. It looms over the characters. When Black queer characters are written into the subject position of culturally Black narratives, questions of identity and belonging tend to take precedence in the storyline, and fears associated with coming out and staying out of the closet feature prominently. On being at once Black, queer, and woman, Joan Morgan writes, "Because of my multiple identities, which locate me and other 'queer' people of color at the margins in this country, my material advancement, my physical protection, and my emotional well-being are constantly threatened."[19] Similarly, in "Bulldaggers, Punks, and Welfare Queens," Cathy Cohen observes that within their "indigenous communities" (read communities of origin), many LGBTQ+ people of color "[recognize] that even within marginal groups there are normative rules determining community membership and power."[20]

While the conditions of Black communal belonging often include the disavowal of queerness, there is evidence in the literary and performing arts that Black queer women artists contend with in-group obstacles, like homophobia and transphobia, in narratives that drift in and through pathos and humor, flagging and waning in and out of moments of joy, disillusionment, pride, and shame. It is also evident in the acts of lovin' on that Black queer women become freer through sharing their complete stories. In my analyses of the works featured in this book, lovin' on is a move toward Black queer women's liberation from the ties that bind them to difficult pasts, allowing them the opportunity to persist in spite of their powerlessness over storms that have left

16. Giles, "Methexis vs. Mimesis," 180.

17. Anderson, *Black Feminism in Contemporary Drama*, 115.

18. Goddard, *Staging Black Feminisms*, 41.

19. Morgan, "Why We Get Off," 34.

20. Cohen, "Punks, Bulldaggers and Welfare Queens," 23.

them in the dark, but which, ultimately, lead them to the promising light of morning. To be clear, lovin' on in BQFP is not all fun and games, nor is it all doom and gloom. The worlds that emerge after the storms in these uniquely personal works are where the cleanup and recovery begin.

Creating sustainable, loving homes and maintaining an orientation toward the future by reckoning with unsustainable pasts in performance allows Black queer women to reconcile periods in their lives (i.e., girlhood) stained by mistreatment. José Esteban Muñoz writes, "Often we can glimpse the worlds proposed and promised by queerness in the realm of the aesthetic. The aesthetic, especially the queer aesthetic, frequently contains blueprints and schemata of a forward-dawning futurity."[21] If Muñoz is right, the utopian possibilities of the textual and embodied performances of multiply queer people are abundant, along with the epistemological possibilities for audiences who entertain utopic and dystopic perspectives of Black queer cultural pasts and presents. Through dramatic and comedic examinations of queer-of-color characters' homes of origin and homes of choice; glimpses into the construction and function of their birth families and chosen families; and explorations of their associated communities' unwritten politics of respectability, BQFP artists tend to depict processes of becoming through lovin'.[22] Such becomings inevitably expose inconvenient truths about Black queer women's positions, roles, and value within the communities they love on most.

Overview of the Book

A Conditional Embrace engages with discourses in Black studies, feminist studies, queer studies, theater studies, and performance studies to examine the archived and publicly accessible works of Shirlene Holmes, Sharon Bridgforth, Staceyann Chin, Donnetta Lavinia Grays, and Dee Rees.[23] Playscripts,

21. Muñoz, *Cruising Utopia*, 1.

22. The definition of *becoming* I invoke here comes from systems theory in social work, which takes a comprehensive view of an individual's behavioral and mental health by evaluating the familial, communal, and societal systems that shape them.

23. While this study is limited to the work of a handful of BQFP artists, countless others write in a similar aesthetic, including Lenelle Moïse (*K-I-S-S-I-N-G*), Donja R. Love (*one in two*), Chisa Hutchinson (*She Like Girls*),Trey Anthony (*Da Kink in My Hair*), Ianne Fields Stewart (*A Complicated Woman*), Nissy Aya (*righteous kill, a requiem*), Tanya Barfield (*Bright Half Life* and *The Call*), Daaimah Mubashshir (*Room Enough (For Us All)*), Christina Anderson (*Good Goods, How to Catch Creation*), Hanifah Walidah (*Bloom* and *Black Folks Guide to Blacks*), C. A. Johnson (*All the Natalie Portmans*), Aziza Barnes (*BLKS*), Maia Matsushita (*House of Sticks and White Mountains*), Tracey Scott Wilson (*Buzzer*), and Angela C. Hall (*Green Light, Magnolia Blossoms,* and *Wife Shop*). Furthermore, Audre Lorde (*The Black*

live performances, and recorded performances serve as primary source materials for this study. Archived interviews with the artists, reviews, essays, playbills, email communications, and playwright's notes are secondary sources. I take seriously the performativity of the text *and* the body in works that document Black lesbian presentation and representation in twentieth- and twenty-first-century US contexts. Each artist featured in the book documents Black queer life by reclaiming rural and urban cultural spaces (i.e., theaters, poetry cafés, coffee shops, clubs, churches, communes) as home; revising history to imagine, reimagine, and adapt Black lesbian narratives for performance; deconstructing stereotypes associated with Black lesbian identity and relationships to represent the range and quality of those performances more accurately; engaging with the concept of the Americas as a geography of comfort and pain for queer women of the African diaspora, thereby acknowledging the influence of environment, culture, and (im)migration on Black queer womanhood and homemaking; and fusing African diaspora, feminist/womanist, and queer aesthetics in their work.

I am especially interested in works in which Black sexual and gender queer women define themselves in their own terms, cultivate and participate in Black *and* queer communities, and love on somebody and themselves as a means of individual and collective survival. The works studied exemplify intersectional artistry as they address overlapping and intersecting issues of race (including colorism), sexual and physical assault, religiosity and hyperspirituality, homophobia, and xenophobia—all of which limit the livability of the protagonists. The works also engage with concepts of motherhood, the Black church, butch-femme, and transnationalism. Reinterpreting style, form, aesthetic, space, time, and language in literature and performance, Shirlene Holmes, Sharon Bridgforth, Donnetta Lavinia Grays, Dee Rees, and Staceyann Chin endow their protagonists with autonomy within imagined circumstances rooted in history, all in an effort to conceptualize and actualize viable models of Black queer womanhood.

The first half of the book explores traditional plays and performance literature. The second half investigates autobiographical performances in solo theater and on film. Chapter 1, "Southern Comfort," presents an analysis of Shirlene Holmes's *A Lady and a Woman* (1990)—a play detailing the romance of two Black women (one butch and one femme) who attempt to raise a family together in a Black Southern town in the 1890s. The women support each other by listening and holding space for one another to grieve past traumas,

---

Unicorn), Alexis De Veaux (*Tapestry*), Jewelle Gomez (*Bones and Ash: A Gilda Story*), Pat Parker ("Where Will You Be"), and Cheryl L. Clarke (*Living as a Lesbian*) paved the way for contemporary BQFP artists.

forgive past wrongs, and move forward together in an oppositional community. An intersectional critical analysis of the play, and the playwright's intent, uncovers a dramatic literary project of reconfiguring gender, sexual stereotypes, and other assumptions associated with Southern Black (queer) womanhood at the dawn of a new century. Holmes's development of new gendered definitions for a "lady" and a "woman" effectively allows her to, as Mecca Jamilah Sullivan writes, "[invent a new language] for articulating Black womanhood in an act of both subjective pleasure and political critique."[24] This chapter marks Holmes as a trailblazer whose lesbian linguistics broke new ground in Southern Black queer dramatic storytelling long before it was common or palatable.

Chapter 2, "Breaking Form," investigates Sharon Bridgforth's Lambda Award–winning performance novel *the bull-jean stories* (1998). A butch mother's liberation story and a butch-femme morality tale, the novel departs from the conventional play structure and format to privilege an Africanist, feminist, queer communal theater experience written in the playwright's signature theatrical jazz style. The chapter opens with an autobiographical meditation on the significance of oral histories in the Black South. After reflecting on the uses of the oral tradition as observed in my grandparents' household in Georgia, I then shift my focus to blues singer Lucille Bogan's 1935 song "B.D. Woman Blues"—a sonic guide to early twentieth-century Black *female masculinity*[25] with its direct, unapologetic declaration of a queer woman's philosophy. Exposing the complexities and contradictions of being a lesbian in the rural South where the church and club overlap, I then turn to *the bull-jean stories* to unpack the butch protagonist's efforts at love and motherhood to critically unfurl Bridgforth's delicate tapestry of Southern Black queer philosophical musings.

Chapter 3, "Girls Like Her," opens with a recounting of the 2003 murder of Sakia Gunn, a masculine lesbian teenager, as she waited with friends to catch a city bus home in New Jersey. Speculating about what the life of a girl like Sakia could have been, I examine the joys and fears of queer girlhood in Donnetta Lavinia Grays's *the cowboy is dying* (2008)—a solo play that depicts Donnetta, a Southern Black lesbian girl struggling with family acceptance, *proper* butch embodiment, and queer homemaking, all while transitioning from adolescence to adulthood, and migrating from the South to the North. I explore the similarities and differences in the journey to womanhood that Donnetta experiences with that of another Black queer girl character named

24. Sullivan, *Poetics of Difference*, 164.

25. This term was coined by Jack Halberstam.

Alike in Dee Rees's film *Pariah* (2011). I identify the distinct connections between the narrative storytelling in both works in animating Black lesbian departures from rigid models of queer gender expression toward personalized, fluid models that reflect a generational shift. I also explore the differing ways that the girls' mothers love on their lesbian daughters at pivotal moments in their development.

Chapter 4, "Making It Solo," continues the exploration of motherhood by analyzing the radical queer feminist acts of lovin' on in the performance poetry and lived experiences of Staceyann Chin—a Jamaican Chinese American lesbian-feminist, solo artist, poet, and activist. Beginning with her origins in slam poetry in New York City in the 1990s, I unpack how Chin's art and life reflect an autobiographical lived performance in which she first conceptualizes and later actualizes semi-utopian home environments in the US and Jamaica. I deconstruct her political poem "Cross-Fire" (2007), reading it alongside her memoir, *The Other Side of Paradise* (2009)—in which she recounts surviving parental neglect, domestic abuse, and sexual abuse as an autonomous girl child and young lesbian woman of mixed ethnicity in Jamaica. I engage with obstacles to Chin's homemaking, including her upbringing, self-imposed exile to the US after being sexually assaulted, and arduous journey to create unconditional love through parenthood and establish a home without borders as documented in the solo play *MotherStruck!* (2015) and the documentary film *A Mother Apart* (2024).

The book concludes with a call for the fortification of Black queer performance by inviting historians, theorists, and practitioners to attend to the dramatic writings and visual narratives of Black queer artists. I include examples of the growing publicly accessible representations of Black queer life to exemplify the potential of recovery efforts—through productions and criticism—to humanize and thoroughly analyze uniquely Black and queer experiences. Considering the growing nuanced dramatizations of Black queer life, I determine that theatrical and cinematic world-makers creating in this aesthetic have been/are imagining progressive and transgressive worlds in which representations and speculations of Black queer personhood are made visible and accessible, flaws and all. If an unconditional embrace equates acknowledgment, public display, and study, I assert that there is no time like the present to rectify what has long been a conditional embrace of Black queer people's contributions to not only Black performance but American performance.

CHAPTER 1

Southern Comfort

The Distinction of *A Lady and a Woman*

In 1990 Dr. Shirlene Holmes (1958–2023) penned a two-act play whose plot centers on two Black women who fall in love in an unnamed Southern town in the 1890s. The dedication in the published script reads:

> For S. Faybell Ma-Hee
> and all the lovers that have to hide.
> Rebecca Ransom: Thank you for "Secrets"
> With courage and pride,
> Shirlene Holmes
> Atlanta, GA
> Oct. 31, 1990[1]

While semi-coded, in this message of thanks Holmes holds queer sisterhood in high esteem in a time and place in which queer sexualities were especially unpopular. In the 1990s, HIV/AIDS was still a global health issue, and discrimination against LGBT people in the US was a common practice supported by legislative policy.[2] Therefore, being out and proud posed a significant threat

1. Holmes, *Lady and a Woman*, 181. Further references to this work are cited parenthetically.

2. A landlord or employer could legally discriminate against LGBTQ individuals by denying them housing or employment. Policies such as Don't Ask, Don't Tell (1993–2011), which

to so-identified individuals socially and economically. There were, however, spaces of comfort for Black queer people in urban cities like New York City, San Francisco, Los Angeles, Chicago, Boston, and Seattle. A lesser-known queer-friendly city was Atlanta, whose feminist bookstores, queer dance clubs and bars, poetry cafés, Unitarian churches, and social clubs allowed Black queer women to gather, conspire, and create.

In a 2013 interview, Holmes explained her motivation for writing *A Lady and a Woman,* saying, "When I sat down, I said, 'I'm lonely. I'll make me a world.' I do that with my writing. If it's not there, I'll put it there."[3] The "not there" she refers to signifies the absence of Black queer women's private lives on stage, an absence contradictory to her experience in artmaking and activism in Atlanta. Hearing her speak of worldmaking, I am reminded of José Esteban Muñoz's characterization of performances of worldmaking as "alternative vistas [which] are more than simply views or perspectives; they are oppositional ideologies that function as critiques of oppressive regimes of 'truth' that subjugate minoritarian people."[4] Holmes's worldmaking "slic[es] into the facade of the real that is the majoritarian public sphere" to elucidate the realities of a Southern Black lesbian subculture in which art and activism coincide.[5]

Holmes's Pride Plays serve as strongboxes for the queer secrets commonly held in the memories of baby boomers (and generations prior) who were forced into closets because of the pathologization of queerness. From 1952 to 1974, homosexuality was documented as a mental disorder in the Diagnostic and Statistical Manual of Mental Disorders (DSM) as published by the American Psychiatric Association. Mid gay liberation movement, the institutional understanding of homosexuality as a disorder was excised from the resource manual and replaced with more nuanced terms like sexual and gender dysphoria. However, this correction did not immediately shift public opinion about same-sex desire. As out queer people became more visible in art, entertainment, popular culture, and politics, the stigma of being queer and being associating with queer people lessened over time.[6] Holmes's Pride Plays encapsulate the "courage and pride" of those living out loud in the "tolerant" 1990s and early 2000s, after generations of being silenced.

---

encouraged gays, lesbians, and bisexuals to be silent about their identities while serving in the military, and the Defense of Marriage Act (DOMA), which reinforced that marriage is legally between a man and a woman, were instituted in the 1990s.

3. Dodds, "Where sex & spirit intersect," 1.

4. Muñoz, *Disidentifications,* 195.

5. Muñoz, *Disidentifications,* 196.

6. LGBTQ+ representation in nineties television, i.e., *Ellen, Will and Grace, Roseanne,* and *The Real World,* exposed the public to more realistic images and narratives of queer life.

In 2016 I sat down with Holmes for a three-hour conversation in her office at Georgia State University in downtown Atlanta. To that point, her impressive life and career—comprising playwriting, prose writing, directing, teaching, and acting—exemplified an intersectional artistry with a focus on identity, culture, and spirituality. Her faith—nondenominational but influenced by a Christian upbringing with beliefs in metaphysics and cosmology—was grounded in a personal truth that, as a six-time cancer survivor, related directly to her mortality. During our discussion, Holmes was undistracted, present, and exceedingly gracious, showing me production photos and videos from her past projects. And without pretense or apology, she discussed her growing collection of short plays documenting Black queer women's lives in the South. While the diversity and breadth of her playwriting is focused on the African diaspora,[7] her Pride Plays and other queer prose, while a modicum of her work, left a mark on Atlanta's queer community in a time when Southern gay and lesbian pride was only a notion.

The late 1980s and '90s, despite the pervasiveness of HIV/AIDS and crack addiction, were exciting decades for queer people in the city. While the majority-white gay and lesbian bars and clubs in Atlanta, including the Eagle, Swinging Richards, Mary's, and My Sister's Room, were more visible, Black queer women also created spaces that enabled them to socialize, organize, and make art to counteract the racism and homophobia outside of the larger queer community, as well as the anti-Blackness and sexism within it. Collectives such as ZAMI NOBLA (the National Organization for Black Lesbians on Aging), Charis Books and More, and popular club spaces like MJQ, Tallulah's, Sports Page, Weekends, Tower Lounge, Rose, and Otherside Lounge became homes to Black queer women—establishments whose pride is reflected in Shirlene Holmes's plays.

Queer theaters, in particular, first embraced *A Lady and a Woman* with its premiere at Atlanta's OutProud Theatre in 1990.[8] Its popularity can be attributed to its romantic storyline, realistic dialogue, traditional structure, two-person cast, and minimal design requirements. The application of realism establishes the central characters, Flora and Biddie, within a Southern geography rife with historical significance, yet other aesthetic elements—like

7. Holmes discussed not only her Pride Plays but her adaptations, including *Caribbean Medea: A Bacchanal,* which premiered in 2014 at Georgia State University, with subsequent performances at the Edinburgh Fringe Festival in Scotland in 2015 and Little Carib Theatre in Trinidad and Tobago in 2017.

8. Productions include those at Impact Theatre Atlanta at Academy Theatre in Hapeville, Georgia, in 2024; Stage Q, Inc. at the Bartell Theatre in Madison, Wisconsin, in 2018; the Department of Africana Studies' Rites and Reason Theatre at Brown University in 2014; and Theatre Rhinoceros at Eureka Theatre in San Francisco in 2013.

spectacle, spirituality, myth, African diasporic cultural traditions, and queer feminist politics—do the work of subtly chipping away at the slice-of-life framework. Lisa M. Anderson finds that the play has "a political focus" that "is *in the situation* [Holmes] dramatizes: black women do fall in love with each other, make lives together, live various gender expressions, and are important parts of black communities."[9] If the "situation" (a same-sex relationship) at the center of the play is the drama, then a same-sex relationship is *always already* in conflict with societal norms. Through testimony and witness, Biddie and Flora excavate the pain of societal rejection and self-imposed isolation through storytelling that, inadvertently, transcribes the historical presence of Black lesbian lovers, heads of household, and community members, and reinforces a minoritarian truth that queer unions have never been fiction.

The South in the 1890s is a questionable playing ground for Black women who pursue sexual freedom, entrepreneurship, and family, but America, itself, is a precarious geography within which to forge viable futures. Thus, the dawn of a new century becomes the perfect setting for Holmes's query about what life would have been like for Black queer women had their lives been valued enough to be recorded. Holmes reflects:

> When I wrote it, it was this meditation I was having about women's lives back in the 1800s and how they negotiated their lives, especially if they were same-sex loving. I wanted to write a play that was about African American women and their lives and about the Southern culture and the folk wisdom. I wanted to address issues about spirituality and sexuality and deconstruct some ideas about how women lived their lives—What's a lady? What's a woman?[10]

Her subjects of study are women of a race and culture familiar to her, yet Holmes is interested in the *untold* histories of these women, an effort resulting in a play that Anderson categorizes as *speculative fiction*—a generative literary approach to imagining the lives of those whose recorded histories are minimal or nonexistent. This term, often attributed to Afrofuturist works, is useful in its pastiche of Black pasts and presents to represent über Afrocentric futures; however, what Holmes and her contemporaries have done is slightly different. Taking archives of the past—stories told and secrets divulged—as source materials, and using a fictional framework to support them, Holmes ruminates about the lives of two nineteenth-century Southern Black women. To meditate

9. Anderson, *Black Feminism in Contemporary Drama,* 111; emphasis added.
10. Holmes, interview, "Theatre Rhinoceros Presents."

on an idea requires fact at its core; thus, based on the playwright's dedication notes, there is less speculation happening than one might think. Holmes hides truths in plain sight, allowing audiences to unpack those truths in their own time. For example, there is no singular historical event that informs the plot; however, during the 1890s, Jim Crow laws were being cemented as a response to Reconstruction-era Black economic and political progress. There is also no white presence (no "white gaze") surveilling the all-Black town in which the characters live, but white folks are, undoubtedly, close by.[11] The system of racism is commented on, suggesting, in a way, that white supremacy is a character, however tangential, but this is not a play about Southern white identity and culture. The absence of white characters is an acknowledgment of segregation practices that kept white and Black communities separate well into the 1960s; thus, their absence reflects a historical truth and convenient plot point that makes room for Blacker and queerer pursuits of Southern comfort.

Biddie's Binary, Self-Naming, and Myths of Strength

Troubling notions of power and gender, the boundaries of butch (masculine) and femme (feminine) are blurred with the introduction of Holmes's alternative conceptual binary of lady and woman (as defined by Biddie in the play). If a lady is a feminine gender and a woman is a masculine gender, then even Flora and Biddie's presentations defy traditional binary assumptions. Biddie is a dark-skinned, "mannish," four-foot-eight butcher, while Flora is a brown-skinned, "buxom," six-foot-tall innkeeper (187). The determinants of feminine and masculine characteristics, here, are visually imperceptible and contradictory; thus, performing lady and woman primarily refers to how they function as cisgender persons within and around the domestic space. This binary concept deconstructs and repurposes butch-femme to elucidate the inner lives of Black women whose obligations to family and community are compulsory. Audiences expecting a traditional butch-femme love story soon discover a complex romance that considers Black queer relationships in the Black South as givens as it proposes two provocative questions: "What's a lady? What's a woman?"[12]

Scholars have written at length about butch-femme gender roles and representation.[13] Since the 1950s, butch and femme identity in lesbian and

11. See Morrison, *Playing in the Dark*.

12. Holmes, interview, "Theatre Rhinoceros Presents."

13. See Sue-Ellen Case's "Towards a Butch-Femme Aesthetic" (1988) to learn about the origins of butch-femme. Read also Jack Halberstam's *Female Masculinity* for an in-depth exploration of complex masculinities within the butch category.

gay culture has been a bold affront to heteronormativity, but Jack Halberstam reminds us that 1970s lesbian-feminists equated butch-femme to "slavish copies of heterosexual roles"[14] rather than, as Anderson reads modern perspectives, "lesbian subject positions or as ways of being (in the phenomenological sense)."[15] Halberstam writes further,

> Female masculinity within queer sexual discourse allows for the disruption of even flows between gender and anatomy, sexuality and identity, sexual practice and performativity. It reveals a variety of queer genders, such as stone butchness, that challenge once and for all the stability and accuracy of binary sex-gender systems.[16]

Biddie's gender binary is unstable, which is the point. By suggesting there is a difference between a lady and a woman, in terms of the premise and presentation of feminine and masculine performance, Biddie inadvertently reconfigures butch-femme to suit her Black lesbian needs. However, the play demonstrates that there is room for the characteristics of ladies and women to shift. To that point, Halberstam, identifying the importance of shifting gender terms and definitions, encourages us to reconsider the "very different meanings in different eras" of female masculinity.[17]

In *A Lady and a Woman,* Holmes considers late nineteenth-century Black lesbians with limited autonomy to be historical heroines who privately rename themselves for themselves while publicly performing gender in more traditional ways. For Biddie, lady and woman exist along the spectrum of lesbian identity and, by unpacking those terms in metaphorical language, she offers Flora more expansive terms with which to identify. It is interesting that she presents this information during their first encounter—a business transaction that takes place in the lobby of Flora's Inn. When Biddie checks in, Flora refers to her as "Miss"—an honorific commonly used for an unmarried woman, or lady. Rejecting the title, Biddie explains: "You're the lady, Miss Flora, I'm a woman. . . . You're the flower. I'm the blade. You seal up and I open up. You the kind that carries and I'm the kind that hauls" (189). A woman, to her, is more masculine than a lady, and a lady is more feminine than a woman. Referencing the symbols of a blade and a flower allows Biddie to instruct Flora, through subtextual clues, that a lady and a woman assume different sexual performance roles: women penetrate and ladies receive penetration. However

14. Halberstam, *Female Masculinity,* 122.
15. Anderson, *Black Feminism in Contemporary Drama,* 104.
16. Halberstam, *Female Masculinity,* 139.
17. Halberstam, *Female Masculinity,* 112.

homonormative her sexual imagination, this is a pivotal moment for Biddie to forward a masculine-of-center perspective about how lesbians get down.

Naming and defining oneself against the norm in an unfamiliar place and in the presence of a stranger is a brave act. Flora's reaction is to pause, indicating an inability to speak. In the silence, Biddie risks judgment that could lead to her being denied occupancy at the inn. Instead, Flora entertains her new tenant's terms. Black feminist scholar Patricia Hill Collins argues, "When Black women's very survival is at stake, creating independent self-definitions becomes essential to that survival" and, moreover, self-definition becomes a "part of the journey from victimization to a free mind."[18] In relaying a radical Black lesbian philosophy, Biddie assumes a liberated positionality from which her perception of self as both masculine and woman becomes possible and enables her to more freely wander in and out of Black communities as a traveling laborer.

There is a direct correlation between Biddie's empowerment and migration. Sarah Jane Cervenak theorizes *wandering* as a "mode of resistance" and liberatory practice of racialized and gendered persons who have been surveilled and punished for deviating from white heteropatriarchal expectations.[19] Wandering is, as Cervenak argues, "a philosophical performance that becomes itself outside of surveillance, outside the four-block restrictions of others' visions and fears of 'dangerous dancing.'"[20] The benefits of Biddie's wandering from town to town outweigh the inherent risks of traveling while Black and female. An explanation for her ability to drift in and through Southern towns with ease is linked to the residents' familiarity with, and dependence upon, migrant laborers who provide essential services. Their perception of her, therefore, takes a back seat to her contributions. The "leather hat, vest and pants" she wears, along with her masculine swagger, denote queerness in the heteronormative spaces she inhabits for work; they are signifiers that put her at risk for surveillance by those who recognize her difference as deviance (186). Yet Biddie manages to navigate these spaces—building houses and butchering animals that sustain and nourish families—by settling temporarily in a given community. It is acceptable for a woman like her to reside among them, but there is an unspoken agreement that she will leave upon completion of her work.

Initially, Flora is suspicious of Biddie, perceiving that something is slightly off (or queer) about her. Flora's height and direct speech endow her with an intimidating air and dominant posture, which prompts the smaller woman to

18. Hill Collins, *Black Feminist Thought*, 123.
19. Cervenak, *Wandering*, 172.
20. Cervenak, *Wandering*, 172.

employ charm as an emollient. Presumably, this is not the first time Biddie has deployed innocuous methods to disarm someone. To be fair, in order to maintain the integrity of her business, it behooves Flora to learn as much as possible about the mysterious tenant. Extending the conversation, she gains insight into Biddie's ethical and philosophical notions about gender and work, information that reassures her that she can pay the rent. When Biddie discloses her occupation, Flora says "that's men's work," to which Biddie retorts, "Not if I get to it first. I'm good. Just have to be. When you're dark and knee high to a duck's ass everything you do better be worth paying for" (188). To survive in a capitalistic society before the industrial and technological ages, her craftsmanship must be exceptional and worthy of fair wages. Because of her queer, petite, and visibly Black presentation, Biddie has overcorrected by making herself physically strong (as strong as a man), but her masculinity and physical prowess are not necessarily linked. On one hand, she has become strong for reasons unrelated to her butchness. On the other hand, Biddie's brawn complements her masculinity, making her, at a glance, more legible as a man when she is on the road. As it pertains to the color of her skin, she has experienced the stigma of being dark-skinned in a country that favors lighter skin due to its adjacency to whiteness. Colorism (an of-color in-group phenomenon influenced by colonization and based in white supremacist ideas and rhetoric) has indelibly imprinted itself upon her and, I argue, pushes her to counter race-based assumptions by laboring harder for the conditional acceptance of the community members she encounters in her travels across the South. Her mental and physical strength serve as armor for the internal battles she contends with as a result of others' negative perceptions of her.

Revelations of past traumas related to colorism, physical abuse, and sexual abuse link Biddie and Flora before their bodies ever come into contact. The arc of their relationship, which morphs from professional to platonic to romantic, is both surprising and seamless, yet, in their first encounter, the sexual undertones in Biddie's declarations and Flora's lack of judgment and noticeable curiosity foreshadow what is to come. While it is unlikely that Flora clocks Biddie's lesbianism, she does recognize the uniqueness of her worldview and is intrigued by the novelty of a woman who arouses her intellectually and, possibly, physically.[21]

For their superficial differences, both are confident, independent businesswomen. As such, it is tempting to label them "strong Black women" types.[22]

21. The stage directions indicate that when Biddie exits, Flora stands silently "watching her in awe" (190).

22. The strong Black woman type is central to many African American plays, including Richard Wright's *Native Son* (1940), Alice Childress's *Wine in the Wilderness* (1969), and Ed Bullins's *Clara's Ole Man* (1965).

Strong Black women are often portrayed persevering through life's cruelest challenges and are held in high esteem for the turmoil they endure. Tamara Beauboeuf-Lafontant finds that strength has become synonymous with Black womanhood, especially in Black communal contexts, and "obliges Black women to exhibit a ready endurance to a life constructed against a backdrop of obstacles, unfairness, and tellingly, a lack of assistance from others."[23] Since they were brought to America in 1619, Black women have essentially served the role of superheroines at the ready for those in need within and outside of their communities, yet there has been little regard for *their* basic care needs.

If a strong Black woman, the "backbone" of her community, shows signs of weakness—if she cries, complains, or refuses to play her race and gender "properly"—others within the community may call her identity as a Black woman into question. Challenges to Black women's authenticity often lead them to lean into performances of strength, embodiments which further inscribe strength as "the defining quality of Black womanhood" while leaving them with limited power over their lives.[24] Beauboeuf-Lafontant observes:

> As a racialized construction of gender, claims of strength by and about Black women not only emphasize their authenticity but their superiority over other women and men based on their abilities to weather all manner of hardship. . . . The normalization of struggle plays a critical role in marking a Black woman's strength so that women without observable or adequate adversity in their lives become contradictory figures.[25]

Innumerable representations of the strong Black woman exist in media. Depictions of Black women distressed and embattled with themselves, others, and situations out of their control reflect a history of African American women's daily struggles with oppressive systems. Notably, contemporary Black women are actively resisting this stereotype due to the immeasurable mental, physical, and emotional cost of the performance. Ahead of her time, Holmes restructures the stereotype by crafting self-sustaining Black women characters who, while carrying substantial traumas in spaces in which their stoicism is expected, show that strength is not an inherent characteristic of Black womanhood, nor is it necessarily aspirational but, instead, can emerge from private subversive acts of self-naming, lovin' on, and being loved on.

23. Beauboeuf-Lafontant, *Behind the Mask*, 71.
24. Beauboeuf-Lafontant, *Behind the Mask*, 1.
25. Beauboeuf-Lafontant, *Behind the Mask*, 72.

Scars, Stretchmarks, and Other Demarcations

Biddie and Flora carry markings, physical and emotional, that represent past events vivid enough for them to recall in the present. And each marking has a detailed origin story. Flora's scars and insecurities are more apparent than Biddie's—she has a scar on her face and stretch marks across her stomach. She becomes visibly emotional when recalling how she got them. Biddie's scars, however, are less visible; they are emotional. Through testimony and witness, an act of lovin' on, they reveal those scars to each other. Flora details her abusive relationship with her ex-husband, which has left a "long keloid scar on the right side of her face" (186). Flora confirms: "That's what happened the night he hit me in my face and I went back into the wall mirror. The doctor wanted to stitch up my face, but I wouldn't have it. When I got my mind back, I was sitting in jail and he was gone" (188). It is clear that she is both a victim of domestic abuse and a fierce survivor. Having been abused by her parental figures, this may have been the first time she fought back against an abuser. This might explain the memory lapse, her refusal to have her face "stitch[ed] up," and her time spent in jail.

While being a "respectable" Black woman matters to Flora, she is not hardwired to accept abuse without responding to it, and there are several ways one might respond. Some people direct their anger inward (toward themselves) and some people direct it toward others. I suspect that, as a child, Flora directed much of her anger and frustration with her parents' maltreatment of her inward (as is suggested by a scene in which Flora recalls the stillbirth of her baby, which I discuss momentarily). Shocked and in pain after the mirror breaks into pieces and slices her face, it is no wonder she loses her mind temporarily and refuses medical care. It is no wonder that she is angry—mad, even. It is no wonder that she finally lashes out toward someone who has hurt her. While such behavior on her part might be considered inappropriate for a lady, it could also be justified by the biblical principle of an "eye for an eye, a tooth for a tooth." Her scar, which she allowed to heal on its own without the aid of a medical doctor to ensure that it healed properly, is a powerful visual reminder and a warning to others that she will fight for her life.

Flora's body, in this play, is a tall, full-figured canvas upon which one could draw numerous conclusions about trauma and power. In *Recovering the Female Body,* Carla L. Peterson writes about the body as a bastion of meaning and perception that can be read in multiple ways:

> When invoking the term "body," we tend to think at first of its materiality—its composition as flesh and bone, its outline and contours, its outgrowth of

> nail and hair. But the body, as we well know, is never simply matter, for it is never divorced from perception and interpretation. As matter, the body is there to be seen and felt, and in the process it is subject to examination and speculation.[26]

Biddie, who finds profound meaning in the ordinary, interprets Flora's scarred face as a thing of beauty, whereas Flora sees it as the aftermath of violence, the cleanup after a storm, ever reminding her of the happening. Peterson continues:

> Perception and interpretation come from different sources. Each of us has a sense of the body we inhabit; but others also look at our bodies and interpret them from their own particular standpoint—coincident with, different from, or supplemental to our own. Initiated from the outside, such perceptions are inevitably partial; nevertheless, we often incorporate them into our own sense of our bodies.[27]

Biddie also perceives Flora's scar as a sign of resilience. Unintentionally objectifying Flora, she says, "It's just like a medal or something. Says you been in the war of life and made it back from the last battle" (188). This discussion allows the body to be a gateway for a deeper connection, one that moves beyond the skin to their inner thoughts—some of which are associated with pleasant feelings and others of which recast them in the roles of prior generations of violated people.

Slaveholders, overseers, and paddy rollers (slave catchers) would enact physical violence against enslaved Black people to punish, tame, and mark them as property; these acts, inevitably, resulted in scarification. In *Beloved* (1987), Toni Morrison's haunting meditation on motherhood and slavery, young Sethe's mother—whom she rarely sees because she labors long on the plantation—tells her that if anything were to happen and Sethe could not recognize her by her face, she could identify her by a mark under her breast—"a circle and a cross burnt right in the skin"—likely representing a Celtic cross symbol—from a branding iron.[28] Similarly, the scars on Biddie's and Flora's bodies are metaphors for suffering, and they reflect and reject a history of centuries of Black women's disempowerment. They represent broken familial bonds of the transatlantic slave trade and broken marital vows (as in, "to love and to cherish"). They symbolize the scars of Black women foremothers that arose from the violence of slavery, intimate partnerships, and even pregnancy.

26. Peterson, "Foreword: Eccentric Bodies," ix.
27. Peterson, "Foreword: Eccentric Bodies," ix.
28. Morrison, *Beloved*, 72.

My reading of Flora's scarred Black body and the "past/passed" bodies of enslaved Black women is informed by Harvey Young's discussion of mid-nineteenth-century daguerreotypes of enslaved people—"silver-surfaced plates polished to a mirrorlike finish onto which images are positively burned and later developed over mercury and fixed with salt solutions."[29] Young explains:

> The capacity of the daguerreotype to serve as a spatial and temporal bridge allows the contemporary viewer to realize that neither race nor the history of "race," as a social concept, is something from which black bodies can easily escape. It does not instantly lose its meaning the moment that a century ends or a new millennium begins. It simply cannot be discarded because ethnologists in the past have employed the term to read black bodies as being different from and inferior to differently colored bodies. The daguerreotype shows us that past events continue to echo in the present. We can see ourselves in the past.[30]

Like Young's reading of the daguerreotype as a repository for and reflection of racialized histories, Holmes's play, too, demonstrates that "past events continue to echo in the present."

For example, the subject of the Black maternal is broached early in the play, catalyzed by a vulnerable moment in which Biddie tells Flora that she found a baby raccoon inside of an adult raccoon that she butchered that day. When she saw it, she began to cry—"The biggest tears run down my face and I was trying to rub them out of the creases of my neck with my free hand" (190)—because it triggered her own desire to be a mother. Flora assures her that there is still time, yet Biddie replies: "You're the one ought to be having the children. You're the lady." (Again, by Biddie's logic, the lady bears children, but the woman provides for them.) Flora, ever confused by Biddie's gender talk, replies, "I declare I don't understand you sometimes. Anyways, I have been down that dead end street and ain't going back. These stretch marks are crawling on me like worms" (191). Holmes, here, masterfully weaves a quilt of text that consists of dichotomous snapshots of motherhood drafted as succinct, necessary moments of lovin' on that propel the narrative from a platonic story to a romantic one. As the sole players, Flora and Biddie have the time and space to engage in intimate dialogue about the historical impact of trauma on Black women's bodies and minds, while offering interventions to the correlative pain.

---

29. Young, *Embodying Black Experience*, 49.
30. Young, *Embodying Black Experience*, 49–50.

Biddie learns that Flora's stretchmarks are marks of trauma that resulted from being impregnated by her stepfather when she was eleven years old. Flora voices responsibility for the death of her stillborn child because on the day she went into labor, a full moon was out, and, in a fit of anger, she cut her hair. A woman cutting her hair represents the end of something or someone. (This is an instance in which we recognize that Flora's spiritual beliefs, or superstitions, help her to make meaning of pivotal events in her life.) It is interesting that, in one breath, Flora asserts her right to defend herself against a violent ex-husband and, in another, she deflects blame from her stepfather onto herself—a move not uncommon for survivors of childhood sexual violence. Her mother's response to her admission of rape is disbelief, which contributes to Flora's adult feelings of guilt related to the stretchmarks. If, as her mother intimates, Flora fits the stereotype of the lying jezebel, then she, even as a child, is always already marked as oversexed and is thereby complicit in her rape, pregnancy, and loss. Despite the physical trauma of the rape, the most painful memory is her mother's repudiation.

Lovin' on Flora in the heart place where she needs it most, Biddie affirms that stretchmarks, like scars, are "a woman's honor"—an assertion that gives Flora permission to love on herself and venture discursively with Biddie to more joyous memories of their mothers. In a scene over tea, Flora deduces, based on Biddie's appetite for peach cobbler, that she has an affinity for peaches. Biddie affirms this: "My mother say she marked me when she was carrying me 'cause it was winter and she couldn't get no peaches when she was craving them" (192). Biddie exposes the peach-shaped birthmark on her stomach. Flora then shows a pineapple-shaped birthmark on her ankle that represents her mother's craving for the fruit during pregnancy—"My mother say she got the pineapple, but it was the next day, so I got this light mark on my leg" (192). This "I'll show you mine if you show me yours" exchange presents an opportunity for Biddie and Flora to connect physically. Although their birthmarks represent lack and punishment, to a degree, in this instance the markings are based in a shared spiritual system of understanding awash with lore and wisdom that strengthens and changes the nature of their bond.

Bedrooms, Bulldaggers, and Black Respectability

At the end of act 1, the couple's lovin' shifts from emotional care to physical pleasure.[31] Having no understanding of what intercourse with women entails,

31. Amber Jamilla Musser writes of Black queer pleasures in her analysis of Janelle Monáe's music video for "Lipstick Lover" from the 2023 album *The Age of Pleasure*. Musser reads it as an

FIGURE 2. Alia Shakira (*left*) as Biddie and Tracey Graves (*right*) as Flora. Impact Theatre Atlanta, 2023. Photograph by Jane Kim.

Flora accepts Biddie's request to "spend the night." Despite her concerns about the potential fallout, she simply does what *feels right,* which Kemi Adeyemi theorizes as "those hard-to-pin-down sensoria signaling that everything has clicked together."[32] The pacing of this scene should be slow as "*BIDDIE wraps her arms around MISS FLORA and kisses her cleavage.*"[33] Startled by this gesture, Flora confesses, "I think I'm starting to . . . love you" (197; ellipsis in original). This admission is not an easy one; she senses that if she reciprocates physically, the consequences of that choice will extend beyond the privacy of their bedroom (see figure 2). "Seem like one of us is gonna get in trouble," Flora says. Ignoring her fear, though, she returns the gesture (197). It is unusual to see Black queer women depicted in erotic situations outside of pornography—an industry that largely fetishizes Black women, othering them with labels like "Ebony" to distinguish their bodies from the unlabeled white bodies that dominate pornographic scenes. The history of the sexualization of Black women's bodies, along with Black women's lack of sexual agency, makes the tender foreplay leading up to Biddie and Flora's lovemaking rather novel,

erotic cinematic "celebration of black queerness" whose primary theme is Black women's erotic freedom. See Musser, "Felt Pleasures."

32. Adeyemi, *Feels Right,* 6.

33. Adeyemi, *Feels Right,* 197. The following quotes are from this page.

even by today's standards.[34] Holmes's rendering of Black lesbian intimacies gives audiences insight into the significance of emotional and physical pleasure in lesbian relationships. Unfamiliar with lesbian sex, Flora admits that she doesn't "know where the parts go." This is understandable. How else would she know how women with female anatomy make each other feel good, let alone reach orgasm? Pulling her close, Biddie assures her: "The parts go just where you want them to. Trust me, you'll know" (197). They get into bed and share a kiss as the lights fade to black, leaving this sexual act of lovin' on to our imaginations.

The morning after, Flora brings up the inevitable scuttlebutt: the townsfolk have been gossiping about Biddie's queerness. It is unclear why Flora has kept this information to herself, but the "talk" has likely been swirling around town since Biddie arrived. In terms of queer clockability, she is an easy mark, but she usually leaves town before the trouble starts. There is a subversive quality to her refusal to alter her gender presentation that she balances with the Southern conformity of keeping her sexuality to herself. The problem for Biddie is that she and Flora are falling in love, a happening that compromises her ability to wander away. Absconding with Flora might be an option, but, in their lifetime, there will be no ideal space for them—no Southern sapphic island of queer womenfolk where they might be together unbothered.

Biddie is not surprised that the townspeople, reading her masculinity as characteristic of lesbianism, suspect she is a "bulldagger." James F. Wilson writes, "Lesbians, who were referred to as 'bulldaggers' and 'bulldyk*s' (or 'bulldyk*rs'), were associated with 'manliness' and masculine clothing."[35] Lisa M. Anderson specifies, "Bulldagger is a label that attaches only to butchness" and can be signified by masculine carriage, clothing, and a short haircut (such as "a very short afro" and "braids or cornrows").[36] Unlike "queer" or "dyk*," "bulldagger," as a term or identity, has not yet been reclaimed by lesbians (although Donnetta Lavinia Grays admirably attempts to do so in *the cowboy is dying,* which I analyze in chapter 3). Notably, SDiane Bogus makes progress in recovering and reclaiming the term in "The Myth and Tradition of the Black Bulldagger." First tracing the etymology of the word and genealogy of the figure, ultimately Bogus calls for Black lesbians of now to "repossess the

34. While Black sexual economies are beyond the scope of this project, Mireille Miller-Young, Nikki Lane, S. Tay Glover, Julian Kevon Glover, and others have written about sex workers in affirming terms, investigating Black queer women subjects who engage in erotic and sexual labor.

35. Wilson, *Bulldaggers, Pansies, and Chocolate Babies,* 7.

36. Anderson, *Black Feminism in Contemporary Drama,* 108.

mode, the lessons, and the power of this unlikely matriarch."[37] Bogus's call to action and optimism lead me to determine that eventually the negative associations with the term will dissipate, but not without a reckoning with its use as hate speech. In the 1890s, the 1990s, and today, the myth of the bulldagger was and is largely negative. "Bulldagger," as wielded in some African American communities, can be a reductive term that ignores variations of *being* among queer women and all but ensures that cisgender queer or questioning women, especially those with a history of heterosexual relationships, like Flora, would rather pass as straight. Increasingly concerned about the religious, social, and material repercussions of her association with Biddie, Flora understands that she will be considered a bulldagger, a marker which would jeopardize her business and social standing.

According to Suzanne Pharr, it is not unusual in heterosexist cultures for women to be labeled lesbians (in the negative sense) for enjoying the company of other women, romantically or otherwise.[38] It has been more advantageous in heterosexist societies to pit women against one another to shore up heteropatriarchy. Heterosexist cultures, regardless of race and ethnicity, assume the power to dictate membership, affording certain rights and privileges to individuals and groups deemed worthy by way of reproducing normative performances of identity. On a micro level, some communities come to a consensus about what is and what is not "acceptable behavior" for its members; these politics extend to the individuals living in those communities. If one cannot abide by the requirements of heterosexuality and gender conformity, they have two choices: (1) wander away or (2) assimilate. As a couple, Flora and Biddie have no desire to leave their community. Instead, they manage to exist as "outsiders-within"[39]—a positionality that affords them insight into (and influence on) the culture in which they live as they resist the constraints of that same culture within the privacy of their queer woman-centered household.

Privacy is key to the maintenance of their relationship as residents of the South. Flora is, in modern terms, a "baby dyk*" and, because of her religious conditioning, it is noticeably difficult for her to process being an outcast (a pariah) in a town in which she is an innkeeper, a midwife, and a spiritual advisor. Thus, she must balance what she understands about lesbianism in

37. Bogus, "Myth and Tradition," 293.

38. See Pharr, "Homophobia and Sexism."

39. See Hill Collins, *Black Feminist Thought.* Collins's research on domestic workers reveals that Black women's work in white households left them "outsiders within" white society. This position gave them unique insight into white society and culture. She also observes that Black women intellectuals and activists have been outsiders-within Black and white societies.

a Judeo-Christian context (that it is wrong for a woman to desire another woman romantically and sexually) with her love for Biddie. In a later scene, "BIDDIE finds MISS FLORA in her room sitting weeping and cracking pecans" (208). The townspeople have begun to fold Flora into their gossip and, as a result, she is having second thoughts about their relationship. An essential member of the community, she is torn between her love for Biddie and maintaining a respectable position in the hierarchy of the community. The catalyst for her melancholy is Cornelia Hooks, who notices Flora wearing what appears to be an engagement ring and asks her, "What you wearing that ring for?" Fearing the loss of respect from her neighbor, Flora lies:

> "I married myself, is that all right with you?" That's what I say back to her, and soon as the words left my mouth, I feel this sharp pain dead in the center of my chest. That's the conviction pain you get when you lying and you know you lying and God knows you lying. (209)

Flora begins to cry again and Biddie soothes her. Riled by Cornelia's offense, Biddie says, "Nobody should be harassing my wife. One of these days I'm gonna lock the door on this place and we ain't never leaving" (209). This, of course, is not a viable option.

In an earlier scene, Flora tells Biddie that the community is gossiping about her (Biddie). Instead of being fearful, however, Biddie demonstrates a willingness to navigate the scrutiny of her racialized community. "They call you a BULLDAGGER WOMAN," Flora says, to which Biddie replies, "That's all right, I'd rather they call me a bulldagger than a ni****. Nothing hurts worse than that" (199). This preference could either indicate that Biddie has internalized her oppression as a sexual minority or conceives racial and sexual oppression hierarchically. If both are taken as givens (and the term "ni****" is not uttered as a racial epithet when used among Black people), then Biddie has faith in the community's potential to tolerate her queerness (in part). She does not, however, have faith in the nearby white community's potential to tolerate her Blackness. "Bulldagger," therefore, is a label that holds far less weight for Biddie than the word "ni****." Still, Biddie understands that she must be strategic in how she publicizes her relationship in order to make a living in the town while lovin' on Flora. "I may need them," she says, "but I ain't gonna let them control when I love and who I love. I'll tell wide behind Cornelia Hooks that you my wife and I'm your wife and that we are happy, and until she respect that don't speak to either one of us again" (209). However noble a perspective and bold a statement, it is easier to assert behind closed doors than it is to proclaim to a straight public.

With homosexuality frowned upon, out or clockable lesbians and same-sex couples in conservative environments are often pressured back into the closet or out of their relationships through shaming tactics, threats of economic insecurity, and threats of violence. That said, Biddie recognizes that it would be reckless to intentionally put their love on display. As the woman, per her definition of such, she is charged with ensuring the safety and comfort of her lady, a protective posture commonly associated with men. While Biddie's power is clearly limited, her words are comforting to a lady whose experiences with the opposite sex have left lasting scars, and who dreads losing her standing in the community. To be clear, in repressive societies, bisexual women and lesbians usually keep their romantic relationships with other women private, preferring that outsiders perceive them as close friends rather than as girlfriends.

Marriage and Motherhood

Black queer women have long mothered unwanted and nonbiological children in their communities, signaling a commitment to the Black community despite its historical disavowal of them. Rather than leave the town for a queer(er) Southern space, Flora and Biddie "disidentify," to use Muñoz's term, with (and in) Blackness to make space for their queerness and reconceptualize the notion of family through a productive approach to queer homemaking. Biddie's vision of mothering a child with a wife is a reality she pines for. However, she cannot do it by herself; Flora's mindset about needing the approval and support of the townsfolk must shift. Biddie encourages Flora to ignore them, arguing that the only permission needed is from God:

> Miss Flora, if you asking people if it's all right for you to love me, you'll be crying a long time 'cause they don't know. The answer ain't in them; it's in you. You only love when God let you; you been free to love me a long time; you just ain't grabbed that freedom yet. (209)

Here, Biddie assures Flora that the love of another and the love of God are interconnected. If God is love, then their love is a holy thing that needs no validation.

By this point, the women are already married in a spiritual sense, but they have not performed a marriage ceremony, a symbolic act that is important to Biddie. Conversely, Flora questions the merit of a ritual binding because (1) it will not be recognized as a legitimate marriage, and (2) she is afraid to marry again because her last marriage ended in divorce. Consequently, she procrastinates, citing the need for prayer as she awaits guidance from her higher power. Biddie challenges Flora's reliance on the supernatural for an answer in this critical moment—"And you gonna pick this same burden up until you look in you 'staeda in your signs and wonders" (210). Taking her portent seriously, Flora concedes.

Initiating an impromptu ritual, Flora spreads her purple apron out onto the floor—"we got to have some purple for under our feet" (211). Purple is a meaningful color, personally and culturally. Flora says, "Purple makes my glory stand out" (197); this relates to the Africanist symbolism of the color purple (a sign of royalty) often featured in African wedding ceremonies. Then, they turn their bodies toward the "south, north, then west and east" (211). Afterward, they pray to "Mother, Father, God" to marry them. Flora's feminism is rooted in the belief that God is neither woman nor man, and always both, which is slightly ironic considering her significant struggle accepting her nontraditional romantic relationship. Combining old and new ideas and traditions, and realizing that she may lose Biddie, Flora commits to her by facilitating a wedding ceremony that solidifies their union as wife and wife.[40]

In Black queer feminist thought, the question of parenthood is a recurring one, and mothering, specifically, of biological and nonbiological children is a topic of both contentment and conflict. Politically, mothering is important because it and other forms of affective labor have been topics of debate in feminism since Black women, like Ida B. Wells Barnett, began contributing to the discourse on women and family during the first wave of the women's movement. In Black feminist discourse, discussions of motherhood are largely investigatory rather than instructive. Alice Walker and bell hooks, in the 1970s and 2000s respectively, questioned the preoccupation of feminists with motherhood while encouraging a feminist approach to mothering. For Walker, that meant having "one child of one's own" and, for hooks, it meant deromanticizing and de-essentializing motherwork.[41] hooks writes:

> It should receive deserved recognition, praise, and celebration within a feminist context where there is renewed effort to rethink the nature of motherhood; to make motherhood neither a compulsory experience for women nor

40. Their marriage is not a legal contract, as same-sex marriage was legalized in the United States only in 2015. Spiritual and symbolic weddings, though, were not unusual among queer folks before the Supreme Court, ruling on *Obergefell v. Hodges*, decided that it was unconstitutional to ban same-sex marriage federally.

41. Many Black feminist thinkers investigate the role of parenting/motherhood in their writing. See Lorde's *Sister Outsider*; hooks's *Feminist Theory*; and Nash's *Birthing Black Mothers*.

> an exploitative or oppressive one; to make female parenting good, effective parenting whether it is done exclusively by women or in conjunction with men.[42]

In *Birthing Black Mothers* (2021), Jennifer C. Nash reexamines motherhood by considering the politics of Black maternal "projects that manifest themselves in myriad ways, ranging from Black peer breastfeeding classes to Black doula trainings, rather than treating Black motherhood as a singular or united space marked by a particular set of political desires."[43] In other words, the continued expansion of Black feminist thought to include alternative perspectives on Black motherhood and mothering are imperative for feminism to remain flexible, open, and relevant to Black women. Lesbian couples, for example, must plot out processes of expanding their families to include children; that meaningful planning, too, can be quite subversive.

Colorism and motherhood converge in *A Lady and a Woman*, as the couple prepares to expand their family. Flora, who is also a midwife, helps deliver a child born to Cora, an eleven-year-old girl, who was impregnated by a family acquaintance—mirroring Flora's childhood pregnancy. After a difficult delivery, the baby girl is born; she is dark-skinned. Flora says, "She ain't black; she's blue black with a shine to her" (217). Cora, who will not even look at the baby, and her parents reject it because of its color. While the primary concern should be that the girl became pregnant at such a young age, unfortunately, the family is most concerned that the child is a less desirable (to them) shade of Black, which speaks to a politics of Black respectability in which skin color matters.

Monique W. Morris defines *colorism* as "a socially constructed hierarchy where lighter-skinned people are perceived as more socially acceptable than darker-skinned people."[44] In this town, social acceptance is a matter of comfort in that the less socially acceptable one is, the less comfortable they are living there. As exemplified in the bulldagger dilemma that Flora and Biddie face before their marriage, membership in the community while being marginalized by it necessitates a *disidentification* with it. Muñoz writes,

> To disidentify is to read oneself and one's own life narrative in a moment, object, or subject that is not culturally coded to "connect" with the disidentifying subject. It is not to pick and choose what one takes out of an identification. It is not to willfully evacuate the politically dubious or shameful

42. hooks, *Feminist Theory*, 136–37.
43. Nash, *Birthing Black Mothers*, 7.
44. Morris, *Pushout*, 22.

> components within an identificatory locus. Rather, it is the reworking of those energies that do not elide the "harmful" or contradictory components of any identity.[45]

The couple in this play are actively engaged in such a "reworking" of injurious "energies" directed toward them from townsfolk like Cornelia, an ongoing process to which they further commit with the adoption of the baby. Cora's family's dismissal of the child is especially poignant to Biddie, who has experienced scrutiny from other Black people because her skin is dark. Conditioned to correlate the child's phenotype with something bad, wrong, and ugly, Biddie's lived experience of girlhood as a dark-skinned person was not a positive one. Yet she has a different vision for this dark child.

The scholarship, literature, and media on colorism in Black communal contexts is substantial, yet the problem persists.[46] To be clear, colorism, like racism, is a pervasive global issue in many cultures, not only Black American culture. As illustrated in a plethora of novels, including Morrison's *The Bluest Eye* (1970) and *God Help the Child* (2015), Delores Phillips's *The Darkest Child* (2004), Lupita Nyong'o's *Sulwe* (2019), and Brit Bennett's *The Vanishing Half* (2020), colorism negatively impacts children's self-esteem, self-worth, and mental health. Biddie can attest to the fact that dark-skinned girls are treated differently from light-skinned girls or even dark-skinned boys based on unfounded ideas steeped in racism that tell us that dark-skinned girls and women are not attractive or worthy of respect and care.

These racist notions of good equating to whiteness/lightness and bad equating to Blackness/darkness have been internalized and passed down through generations of Black families and communities. And although the biases may be conscious or unconscious, the latter is the most dangerous because ignorance does not allow for reflection in the moment or accountability for holding false perceptions up as truth and perpetuating such falsehoods about skin color and value. Even Flora and Biddie, in their outcast state, show concern about the baby's skin color and speculate about how she came into the world so "Black," as if it is a problem that needs solving. The baby's color is almost alien to Flora, who comments that the baby is "just as sweet and Black. I mean the chile so Black she blue. Seem like when you hold her, it's like having a piece of coal in your hand. You think some the Black gonna come off on you when you put her down" (216). While this description is beautiful, both women are concerned for the child's well-being in a colorist community.

---

45. Muñoz, *Disidentifications*, 12.

46. For more on colorism, see Wilders's *Color Stories*; Russell-Cole et al.'s *Color Complex*; Norwood's *Color Matters*; and Kerr's *Paper Bag Principle*.

Leaning on folklore, as they did when discussing their markings, they toss ideas around as to the cause of the child's "condition," determining that little Cora drank too much coffee ("Strong too, with lots of sugar and no cream)" (217). This explanation is one of many myths of colorism that circulated in Black communities post slavery, and although mythical beliefs steeped in colorism have long been a part of African American life, underneath the humor lies a damaging notion of cause and effect that negatively marks dark-skinned people. Through affirmative dialogic speech between the two women, without reflection on the origins and construction of such a myth, the damaging idea at its core (that one can be "too" Black and that someone or something is always to blame) is reified culturally to racist ends. Some of the "preventative measures" to ensure that a baby would not be "too" dark might include lightly pinching their nostrils so that the nose might appear smaller (more European) or encouraging a child to stay out of the sun so as not to tan. Although these notions and practices are symbolic of internalized racism, they were also an attempt by African Americans to assimilate to a white-dominant society after slavery: an attempt to become a part of a white national culture within which their comfort was never intended. European standards of beauty, which, again, are associated with privilege and value, influence Flora and Biddie's discussion of the child's deep skin tone and subsequent decisions about childrearing in a colorist community and racist society.

Dreams, or Innervisions

Deciding to raise the child themselves, as queer women have historically done, their union, gender roles, and respective life histories prepare them to parent an abandoned child in an antagonistic world. Establishing a family unit rooted in love and acceptance, both women make a commitment to one another to embrace the child without conditions. Flora vows to "make sure she's a lady" and Biddie vows to "make sure she's a woman," essentially proposing an intention to raise a well-rounded girl/woman with feminine and masculine skills and qualities by which she will live and make a living (218). And that is the point: not to survive but to live. Understandably, the idea of survival commonly arises in feminist movement discourse, as girls and women globally have long been denied access to education, freedom of speech and bodily autonomy, economic resources, and opportunities for advancement in business and property ownership. Those freedoms, which even in the "land of the free" are not rightfully guaranteed, could only have been dreamed up by the likes of Flora and Biddie and their foremothers.

Based on Shirlene Holmes's project of "making [herself] a [Southern Black queer] world" with this play, she not only loves on generations of foremothers, but she loves on the woman she is in 1990 who is, then, conceiving a play for future generations of queer folk. *A Lady and a Woman* is a documentation of cultural practices in the communities to which Holmes belongs, and it is an articulation of her dreams for them. The inevitable encounters between Black straight bodies and Black queer bodies in the story reshape and reconfigure (from the inside out) a community from one that disapproves of unruly girls, fighting women, and queer folk to one that must deal *with* them. Through a radical love practice that does what it claims (loves on), the Black queer presence in the play (as represented by Flora and Biddie) disrupts notions of what "Black is" and "Black ain't" (to invoke the premise of Marlon Riggs's 1994 documentary film). Holmes makes space in the South for what is and what has always been culturally Black by reclaiming contentious spaces for Black queer visibility and livability.

With its continued production, it is clear to me that *A Lady and a Woman* has had a positive impact on theater-makers and audiences who meet the work where it is (where and with whom Holmes situates the action, structures the dialogue, and guides the story), leading me to deduce that a solo dreamer *can,* through the theatrical medium, expand the possibilities of Black queer presence and performativity in immediate and affecting ways that linger in the bodies of those performing, in the bodies of witnesses to the performance, and on the stages upon which the performance takes place. Although theater is generally far less profitable and accessible to audiences than, to use Phillip Auslander's term, "mediatized" productions (film, television, digital media) are, theater relies heavily on "liveness" to make and remake embodied memories.[47] Theater is an underutilized artistic medium for Black queer visibility but is as affecting as more popular artforms because of its reliance on a human exchange of energies between bodies in real time. As Holmes's groundbreaking play shows, as does Sharon Bridgforth's jazz-inspired blues novel, *the bull-jean stories* (see chapter 2), theater provides opportunities to engage with the many complex faces of Black life and love.

By lovin' on one another, Biddie and Flora actualize each other's wildest dreams. Recognizing Biddie's contributions to her life, primarily giving her permission to be soft (and ladylike) after a hardening life—a privilege that Black women have rarely been afforded—Flora thanks her wife for making her dreams come true. Confidently shrugging the compliment off (considering that words of affirmation or negation can impress themselves on the body

47. For more on liveness, see Auslander, *Liveness.*

and that body can choose to receive or reject them), Biddie says, "I don't believe in dreams; this is a vision and I seen it all along" (220). Biddie's vision is predicated on her lady/woman binary, which enabled their relationship to find firm ground and ignited their mutual reckonings with bodily and emotional trauma to create space for joy and deeper experiences as friends, lovers, wives, mothers, businesswomen, and active community members. The two could certainly have lived out their days as a content, childless couple; however, they had the desire to become parents. Therefore, by the time the opportunity presented itself, they had done the healing and wellness work to take in a "problem" child that, they, as "problem" mothers, had the capacity and means to parent. By lovin' on each other and somebody else, they manifest an ideal family for themselves that can thrive within a conservative Southern space and time, although surely not without challenges.

A Lady and a Woman documents the lives of the "funny" Southern ladies and bulldagger women who peeked in and out of closets with a wink and a smile, or stood in the doorway with fear and trembling. The ones who maneuvered their way through red clay terrain to get to work, to club meetings, and to church meetings on time. The ones who wandered and ran through forests filled with Georgia pine trees with their babies strapped to their backs and bloodhounds on their trails. The ones who fought back, if they could, their faces bloodied and bruised by those who swore to love them. The ones who remained in communities they built with bare hands and open arms. It is a story for Black and queer folk who have cried at the sky, prayed for a sign, remained steadfast in their purpose, and dreamt new dreams to take the place of old nightmares.

CHAPTER 2

Breaking Form

Orality, Blueswomen, and Theatrical Jazz in *the bull-jean stories*

In her study of post–civil rights era performance, *Black Movements: Black Performance and Cultural Politics,* Soyica Diggs Colbert unpacks existing theories of Black performance and performativity, including those of Anita González, D. Soyini Madison, and Thomas F. DeFrantz, to conceive a framework through which to analyze past political movements through contemporary artistic invocations and interpretations. Expanding these theories, Colbert writes:

> While I do not suggest that texts perform, I do argue that representations of performances function as a part of the archive of a performance and expand the social, imaginative, political, cultural, and aesthetic possibilities of the enactment. To represent the oral quality of storytelling in the novel, as Toni Morrison does in *Song of Solomon* (1977), is to provide insight into the particular characteristics of Black expressive culture.[1]

Taking Colbert's claims as inspiration, in this chapter I focus on Sharon Bridgforth's first performance novel *the bull-jean stories* (1998)—an archival project that, in text and performance, preserves a singular Black queer feminist story told in the oral tradition from multiple Black queer perspectives. Like Colbert, it is not my intention to argue whether texts actively perform or not. I, too,

1. Colbert, *Black Movements,* 17–18.

agree with González and DeFrantz, who situate performance in the body, and assert that "[performance] is created by living [breathing] people."[2] However, when analyzing the elements of Bridgforth's writing style and musical aesthetic, I find the remarkability of the text on the page to be due, in large part, to the visual performance of the language on paper. Having spent years looking at the letters, words, punctuation, typeface design, spacing, and syntax of this novel, I am convinced that the text does something akin to performance. An exploration of Black queer women's memories through orality, *the bull-jean stories* is an affecting work that defies tradition as it embraces the intersecting cultures, identities, and histories of Southern Black queer women folk.

The next section opens with a meditation on memory that illustrates the significance of the oral tradition in Southern Black culture. An autobiographical contemplation, it serves as an opening through which I contribute to discourses on the role and function of the "everyday" griot in Black communities. It is important to me, as a woman of the South, to make connections between my own experience of orality as an act of lovin' on oneself and somebody else to more authentically and thoroughly investigate the performances of lovin' on in Bridgforth's complex yet accessible work of performance literature.

Everyday Griots

In my paternal grandparents' home in south Georgia, the elders regularly recalled stories about our family in the den—one of the few spaces we could all congregate since Grandmama would not allow us children in her pristine, yellow-hued, 1970s-style dining room. In that coveted space reserved for holidays, graduation celebrations, and other special occasions, stories and storytellers were plentiful. Some regaled the room with observational humor, and others with a dramatic delivery that resolved into quiet contemplation. When our large family communed, stories of all kinds flowed like sweetened iced tea. Anyone of adult age could interject with a detail or make a correction to the story, the result of which became a series of strung together memories that culminated in a somewhat-cohesive glimpse into our family's history. A homebody, I would sit nearby eavesdropping on the adults while they cooked and talked. Occasionally, they would talk among themselves in veiled terms but, more often, the stories recalled were child-friendly. Over decades of listening, even passively so, they became my own.

2. DeFrantz and González, *Black Performance Theory*, 6.

When my mother tells the story of how "Old Blessing"—my paternal great-grandfather George L. Tift—"saved my life" as an infant, I visualize my then-four-year-old brother attempting to get rid of his baby sister for good as he holds a starched white pillow over my face as I lay sleeping. Envisioning the details of the pink room (now green), representative of my grandmother's sorority, and the faux walnut wood bedpost (now gone), I imagine my mother tiptoeing in the hallway at Old Blessing's gentle suggestion—"Daughter, go see what that boy's doing back there [because] he's awful quiet." She peeps through the door and quickly leaps to my rescue. My mother has told me this story with such consistency and simplicity that I now tell it with a similar ease and fondness. Now the elder version of her young heroine self, she accesses the comedy in the dramatic memory; the immediacy of the moment has long dissipated and the feelings associated with the initial sighting of my brother, the pillow, and me are no longer key to its telling. While my mother is the active character in this story, I marvel at the ancestral transfer of knowledge from grandfather-in-law to granddaughter-in-law then from mother to daughter. This is a story and a memory we *share.*

In the Black South, storytelling has played a major role in maintaining families and building communities. As I suggested in chapter 1, sharing stories from one generation to the next is an act of loving on one's chosen family. While many of those stories are difficult to tell, recall, or remember, the act of storytelling has fortified family units through the establishment of bonds dependent more upon shared memory than shared biology. *Orality* is how Southern African Americans who are descendants of enslaved people, many of whom have scattered records of their family histories, have transferred and retained memory and knowledge. A group or solo effort, orality is performance-as-epistemology, and the *griot* is compelled to divulge what they know to those who need the information most. Reflecting on the role and impact of the griot—the keeper and conjurer of stories (an elder)—Daniel Banks writes, "The ritual utterer of words conjures time; they know how to stop and start time through the histories they impart and also through the re(creation) of those histories."[3] The ritual utterer in a family unit, the one who tells (and retells) stories, tends to be the oldest living relative, and when they pass down (or pass on) stories with intention, that history continues in the imaginations of their descendants.

My paternal grandfather Jesse James Tift, the oldest of Old Blessing's two sons, was such a griot. Years before his death, I recorded some of our conversations. StoryCorps Griot, a nonprofit initiative committed to preserving

3. Banks, "Hip Hop Theatre Initiative," 143.

and sharing the experiences of everyday people through dialogue, inspired my recorded talks with him. Energized and animated when we talked about the Tifts of African descent who lived in and around the city of Albany, he would utilize props—the map of the state of Georgia or a small, green-lined notebook with our family tree hand-drawn on its pages—to edify me. He was a natural storyteller known for his generally quiet, yet imposing nature, but if you wanted answers from him, you *had* to ask questions. I hung on every word, trying not to interrupt him. If I asked follow-up questions to fill in the gaps where a detail was missing, it seemed to assure him that I was listening closely, and he would continue talking. We engaged in conversations about race, economics, politics, society, and culture, after which I would leave feeling an immeasurable sense of pride to be his grandchild.[4]

In retrospect, I wish we could have discussed our "sweeter" kinfolk, but, in the South, queerness is not commonly spoken of—at least not with ease and fondness. Realistically, it was a conversation we never would have had; it would have been improper to speak of gender and sexuality with an elder of the Silent Generation. Men born during the Great Depression in the rural South, generally spoke, if at all, of "queers" and "bulldaggers" in the derogatory sense, as in jest, but certainly without consideration or identification.[5] The South is not a region one readily thinks of when imagining a history of Black queer joy or allyship, but queer people have always resided there. In *Black. Queer. Southern. Women* (2018), E. Patrick Johnson invests in this fact in his excavation of Southern Black lesbian and bisexual women's oral histories. Of these stories and the historical presence of queer Southern folk, Johnson writes, "Sometimes stories are like honey: slow to pour. Once it gets started, though, it's hard to stop. Its stream of luscious gold covers lots of ground, ignoring boundaries as it sticks to and spreads over surfaces."[6] Johnson's comment on the elusiveness of time and its potential to set historical records straight acknowledges the transformative potential of storytelling. Once an authentic story "gets started," the stories (and its griots) continue to flow.

Sharon Bridgforth's *the bull-jean stories* is a Lambda Award–winning work lauded for centering Southern Black lesbian bodies and voices at a time when

4. It is difficult to fathom how the Black residents of Albany—who have represented the majority racial demographic in the city since the mid-1800s—survived enslavement, Reconstruction, and Jim Crow segregation.

5. To be clear, I never heard my grandfather utter either of these terms in any context, which supports my point that silence around queer folk, who have always existed, is a cultural practice that has and continues to contribute to the erasure of Black queer histories.

6. E. Johnson, *Black. Queer. Southern. Women*, 15.

there was minimal representation in literature and drama.[7] Since its original publication and the premiere of its theatrical adaptation *blood pudding* (in the same year), the poetics of bull-dog jean, the central character, continue to inspire new generations of readers and audiences. This novel offers up early twentieth-century Southern Black lesbian masculinity and butch-femme romance without preface or apology through a character-driven story that reinforces that Black queer people have long existed in the Bible Belt.

The Black church and the club are spectacular sites in the novel, in part and at once, representing refuge and danger, bitter and sweet, queer and straight. Readers and audiences are invited to step through the wide-open doors of the juke joint—a sacred, inviting social space for even the straightest of queer folks to gather, dance, drink, and partake in the blues. As Ramón H. Rivera-Servera observes, the club can arm queer folk of color with strategies "to navigate homophobia and racism outside of the club."[8] The Black church, which is, indeed, outside of the club, is, *in bull-jean,* a contentious space of confirmation and rejection for the amorous butch lesbian subject. Regarding the symbiosis and symbolism of the secular and nonsecular in her writing, Bridgforth admits, "Queer and trans people are holy people in my work. So I situate the juke joint as a holy site. So the same things that you see in a grove or in a Black church when its [*sic*] swinging, it's what's happening in the juke joint."[9] Community, family, jazz, and the sacred are endemic to the spirit of her writing and performance work. As Omi Osun Joni L. Jones details in *Theatrical Jazz: Performance, Àṣẹ, and the Power of the Present Moment,* Bridgforth's creative process is as life-affirming and life-changing for the writer as it is for those who witness the work which, like its creator, is always in progress. *Spirit* is in the story, text, and embodiment—and Bridgforth, like Holmes, embraces the notion that spirituality is a birthright of Black queer people rather than an aspect of Black culture that is to be avoided or made inaccessible to them.

In *Mouths of Rain,* Briona Simone Jones informs us, "Black lesbians have reconstructed and redefined spirituality, memory, afterlife, conjure, and ritual. Whether through praxis, prayer, supplication, or the convergence of all three, the connection to the divine has remained salient."[10] Jones's affirmation about the constructedness and fluidity of divine ideas, religious and spiritual practices, and the limits and depths of what can be known about the human and spiritual experience reminds me of something my grandfather once said.

7. bull-jean first appeared in Bridgforth's *lovve/rituals & rage*—an installation first performed in 1993 by The root wy'mn Theatre Company, which she founded.

8. Tift, "Review of *Performing Queer Latinidad,*" 312.

9. Royster, "Queering the Jazz Aesthetic," 537.

10. B. Jones, "Introduction," xxviii.

Unsolicited, he commented on the tension between the church and the club, drawing upon visible contradictions plucked from the world around him. Plainly, quietly, and in a matter-of-fact delivery, he said: "Krissy, folks'd be drunk in the juke joint on Saturday then be in the church praisin' the Lord on Sunday." Then he laughed to himself a knowing laugh—a laugh that intimated that the separation of the secular and religious was not abided by a good number of Black Southern folks—many of whom carefully navigated their way through the church and the club to remain in step with the social expectations of both spaces.[11] Their devotion to Black cultural forms of expression in those spaces illustrates that religious and secular lovin' existed simultaneously with quite a bit of overlap.

Bogan's Blues

Art and politics are rarely separate in Black women's movement work, and the desire for social change is intersectional, immediate, and future-oriented. In the 1935 blues song "B.D. Woman Blues," singer Lucille Bogan (who released the song under the name Bessie Jackson for anonymity) belts: "Comin' a time, B.D. women[12] ain't gonna need no men / Comin' a time, B.D. women ain't gonna need no men / Oh the way they treat us is a lowdown and dirty sin."[13] Throughout most of the song, Bogan sings in the third person. Yet the singular use of the pronoun "us" suggests that she, too, is a "bulldagger" woman—one who enjoys the company of women. The mistreatment she documents in this first verse feels personal, foregrounding a specifically lesbian "problem" with patriarchal oppression. Then, she proposes a radical separatist intervention. The concept of lesbian separatism, as expressed by Black lesbian-feminists like Cheryl L. Clarke in the 1980s, is, in retrospect, what Bogan portended decades earlier.[14] Traveling blueswomen like Bogan, Bessie Smith, and Gertrude "Ma" Rainey—all of whom painted explicit, "good time" soundscapes with lyrical references to sex and substance use in their music—had backstage

11. For a stellar depiction of the significance of the rural juke joint and its legacy of blues music, see Ryan Coogler's 2025 film *Sinners*.

12. B.D. is an acronym for "bulldagger" or "Bull Dyk*"—a colloquialism commonly used in the South and, often, an epithet for a same-gender-loving woman or lesbian. In other parts of the US, the term "bulldyk*" might be used instead.

13. Bogan, "Lucille Bogan—B.D. Woman's Blues," 19.

14. See Avilez, "Movement in Black." Of Clarke's poetry, GerShun Avilez writes, "Through her poetic mapping of urban spaces, Clarke details the kinds of violence that racial and sexual minorities face and that create feelings of spatial alienation because of being denied access to the social world" (23).

and centerstage views of the queerer happenings in the club—some of which, it is said, they participated in. Little is known about Bogan's personal life; however, the song's authenticity and self-referentiality suggests an intimate understanding of the "rough" (read butch) lesbian archetype of her time. This song, in part, brings attention to the lesbian as a gender and sexual minority. It also attends to the potential of butch women's empowerment to dismantle gender and sexual oppression.

Of the radical futurism of Black lesbian thought, Briona Simone Jones writes, "Black lesbians construct a new politic; one wherein coalitional politics and ending all forms of oppression for everyone are at the forefront of their liberatory discourses and practices."[15] Having an informed, nonperformative Black lesbian feminist ethics, then, leads Black lesbians to argue for the rights of *all* oppressed people in their work, a wholistic arts-activist approach to changemaking typical of Black women poets. In "Lesbianism: An Act of Resistance" (1981), Clarke writes: "No matter how a woman lives out her lesbianism—in the closet, in the state legislature, in the bedroom—she has rebelled against becoming the master's concubine. . . . This rebelling is dangerous business in patriarchy."[16] And it *is* dangerous. Clarke documents her own voyage in poetic form with radical flare in *Living as a Lesbian* (1986). Therein, she reflects on the pros and cons of living queerly out loud and calls for reform regarding such issues as racial and gender-based violence, thereby demonstrating that living in and lovin' on bodies that are Black, queer, and female-presenting, amorously or nonamorously, are acts of protest.

the bull-jean stories is such a poetic protestation in which public performances of gender and sexual queerness by racialized bodies exemplify the emancipatory possibilities of lovin' on for an individual and a collective. In the opening to *bull-jean & dem/dey back,* Mary Anne Adams, an activist, social worker, and founder of Atlanta's ZAMI NOBLA (National Organization of Black Lesbians on Aging), recalls her first encounter with Sharon Bridgforth and the novel's characters during a public reading held at Charis Bookstore in Atlanta in 1999. Adams writes, "She gave us a lyrical trove that held us spellbound, and wove a magical tale of the rural south, unapologetic same-sex attraction and bad-ass Black women who lived by the rules they made."[17] Having had a similar experience "in Austin, Texas in a small theater, sometime in the '90s," playwright and director Virginia Grise recalls: "That day I witnessed something I had never seen before. I've heard some people call it church but I ain't ever been to a church like that. It was rowdy and loud, raucous and

15. B. Jones, "Introduction," xxvii.
16. Clarke, "Lesbianism: An Act of Resistance," 126.
17. Bridgforth, *bull-jean & dem/dey back,* 13.

ratchet and tender all at the same time. . . . And all of it—so damn queer, and Black and Southern."[18]

Bridgforth's imaginings of the lives of Black lesbians who were unable to be open about their queer gender and sexual identities is an homage to prior generations, the stories of whom were not written down, memorized, or passed on. She writes:

> though I can't dictate their particular words
> i do understand that the voice of **the bull-jean**
> **stories** belongs to them. these are the stories
> they didn't tell me the ones i needed most.
> bull-jean is the butch/southern/poet/warrior
> wo'mn hero *i wish i'd known.*[19]

While there are few recorded histories of Black lesbians in the 1920s from which to draw inspiration, there were queer blues songs—like "B.D. Woman Blues" and Ma Rainey's "Sissy Blues" (1926) and "Prove It to Me" (1926)—whose lyrics, at the least, leave breadcrumbs from which artists like Bridgforth can make a meal. Like the blues, jazz has been a unique source from which playwrights have mined stories, proposed questions, and responded to aggravations in the form of love notes, often written in shortform.

Notes on Theatrical Jazz

Bridgforth's theatrical jazz aesthetic takes its lead from Black sonic-inspired writing styles such as Aisha Rahman's jazz aesthetic. A Black Arts movement playwright, Rahman is best known for *The Mojo and the Sayso* (1989) and *Unfinished Women Cry in No Man's Land While a Bird Dies in a Gilded Cage* (1977). The latter is a short, dense "polydrama"—a collision of two storylines within one play—that exemplifies the potential of the jazz aesthetic to illuminate the logics of life and death.[20] Notably, Yoruba cosmological epistemologies inform the playwright's belief that there exists three concordant worlds—the unborn, the living, and the dead—a premise that gives her room

18. Bridgforth, *bull-jean & dem/dey back*, 83.

19. Bridgforth, *the bull-jean stories*, preface (emphasis added).

20. I directed a production of *Unfinished Women* at Vanderbilt University in 2022. The experience conceptualizing, directing, and performing in (unexpectedly) this work was challenging yet memorable. Once the cast of undergraduate students found the musicality of the piece, the disparate stories of the girls and Bird began to connect.

to write way outside of the lines of the well-made play. First produced in 1977 at the New York Shakespeare Festival, the play's structure, form, and language defied the performance expectations of modern Western audiences to privilege an Africanist point of view and an African American jazz poetics, while presenting the everywoman/girl as protagonist.[21]

Set on March 12, 1955, the play juxtaposes a day in the life of five unwed, pregnant teenagers with the final day in the life of bebop saxophonist Charlie "Bird" Parker. With studied attention to phrasing, repetition, revision, tonal shifts, and timing, Rahman's writing interpolates Parker's playing style. Like the notes of the minor bebop scale, the text is rooted yet unstable. As Parker loses his grip on reality, so does the play. The personal narratives of five pregnant girls living at Hide-a-Wee Home for Unwed Mothers pour forth on the day they must decide to keep or give up their babies for adoption. Concurrently, Parker gets high (on drugs and memories) in the luxury boudoir of his white European girlfriend, Pasha. Parker's music is the glue between the discordant plots; it merges his inevitable demise with the girls' difficult decisions. What is most interesting to me about this play is the girls' love for Bird. Listening to the radio, their only connection to the outside world, allows them to suspend their dreams on every note, as if his saxophone could transport them away from their problems. The love the girls have for him represents a freedom beyond their grasp, but as long as the music continues to play, there is a chance for them to return to a past when they were not expectant mothers but simply teenagers.

The play ends in a group sonic eruption of repeated and overlapping utterances, improvised sounds, movements, and gestures reminiscent of the improvisation of jazz and the moans of blues and gospel. While bebop was considered an "experimental" form when introduced by Parker and Dizzy Gillespie, it soon became popular among musicians who wanted to express themselves in ways that transcended notes, octaves, and time signatures. The jazz aesthetic, which continues to be adapted, reconfigured, and repurposed by dramatists, enables audiences to interact with the performers as they, with a partial or completed script, explore critical intersectional inquiries of important social issues.

Bridgforth's theatrical jazz aesthetic, as theorized and facilitated in her and Omi Osun Joni L. Jones's work with the Austin Project, is not only a dramaturgical tool but a collaborative approach to theater-making, which they describe as "an African American art creation [composed of] virtuosity, improvisation, being present, listening, witnessing, expansion, and exploration of time,

21. For an in-depth analysis of the play, see Kroger, "Jazz Form and Jazz Function."

polyrhythms, non-linear forms, breath, synchronicity, and transcendence."[22] The invocation of spirit in Bridgforth's work is meaningful and symbolizes a desire to capture essential "truths"—those which one knows are true because they arise from their own spirit. Bridgforth and Jones write: "It [the jazz aesthetic] necessitates the fact that when the individual works from a place of deep truth, works hard to achieve an advanced level of craftspersonship, and unmasks, unleashes, and reveals spirit, the individual is able to hear more deeply and therefore is better able to create in concert with others."[23] Bridgforth assigns the jazz aesthetic a female aura, describing it as active and "about revolution/the revolution of spirit."[24] Jones posits that the jazz aesthetic "is at its best used for the purpose of building, nurturing, extending, and celebrating the humanity, liberation, and dignity of all people globally."[25] Hence, the theatrical jazz aesthetic is a performance modality and method based in activism and coalition-building between women and other marginalized people to help them find voice and claim space through the development of identity-based works.

Bridgforth's *dat Black Mermaid Man Lady* (2018), *River See* (2014), and *delta dandi* (2010) are such works that foreground "black [queer] heroism and cultural values by tapping from ritual designs, musical and dance patterns, and themes influenced by an African world-view."[26] With the early influence of Laurie Carlos on Bridgforth's theatrical training, ritual movement, dance, and gesture suffuse her performance installations. Cyclical temporality is also an Africanist element she applies to her narratives. For example, Jones observes that the character Gurl "appears again and again in Bridgforth's work" and is representative of the playwright "working through childhood trauma to achieve adult peace."[27] In *delta dandi,* with the help of other African descendant-characters who hold powers and properties of the *orisha* (Yoruba deities), Gurl "work[s] through many lifetimes of abuse" that arise out of racist and heteropatriarchal conditions.[28]

Fusing Africanist, feminist/womanist, and queer themes, Bridgforth consistently adds queer gender identities in the worlds she dictates. In the script

22. O. Jones et al., *Experiments in a Jazz Aesthetic,* 15–16.

23. O. Jones et al., 16. On August 12, 2016, I participated in a three-hour workshop—"The Theatrical Jazz Workshop"—facilitated by Dr. Omi Osun Joni L. Jones, at the Association for Theatre in Higher Education conference.

24. O. Jones et al., *Experiments in a Jazz Aesthetic,* 15–16.

25. O. Jones et al., *Experiments in a Jazz Aesthetic,* 16.

26. O. Jones et al., *Experiments in a Jazz Aesthetic,* 16. I insert "queer," here, because this aesthetic and identity is central to Bridgforth's work.

27. O. Jones, *Theatrical Jazz,* 122.

28. Bridgforth, *delta dandi,* 187.

for *delta dandi,* she instructs that Baba (father) should "be played by an identifiably gender queer person," and Conductor, an optional character, should "be a woman or identifiably gender queer."[29] (Bridgforth sometimes plays the Conductor in her productions, and rather than directing her installations, she "composes" them.)[30] Africanist communal storytelling, with Bridgforth performing the griot role, encourages orality. Not only is a historical narrative being told by the performers ("improvisers") to the audience, but the audience, as "active witness/participants,"[31] work with the performers by reading aloud dialogue given to them by the Conductor. By "helping to create a soundscape," the audience co-produces Gurl's journey as she moves through time and space, allowing them to bear witness to her struggle as a multiply marginalized person and to help (through improvisation) usher her home to a loving reality far different from her ancestral past.[32] Audiences, to be clear, do not sit idly by observing Gurl's journey; by virtue of being present, they are encouraged to participate. In this way, the differences (if any) between them and the characters are insignificant to the work they do together to tell Gurl's story.

Bridgforth's jazz writing style and inclusive intent lay the theatrical ground upon which a blues-singing, gender queer, lesbian folk hero, like bull-jean, can stand. The literary form of *the bull-jean stories* is the performance novel—a "[text] that [is] written both to have a life on the page and to be read aloud or performed onstage."[33] This form, in terms of process, represents "the jumping-off point" from which the playwright "excerpts" (or adapts) the novel into a text drafted for performance.[34] A Black Southern dialect is the language of the novel—a shared expressive parlance between the straight and queer characters. To follow the story, the witness/participant must adapt to its vocality and musicality, which is reflected in Bridgforth's phrasing and placement of words and marks on the page. For example, bull-jean's voice is emboldened with the zigzagged placement of her dialogue connoting emotion. Italics, lowercase lettering, slashes, phonetic word spellings, punctuation, and spacing are strategically placed throughout the text.[35] They are elements of a code that signifies a language or mother tongue ascribed to Bridgforth's Southern queer characters.

29. Bridgforth, *delta dandi,* 187.

30. Bridgforth acknowledges the inherent musicality of both her texts and the bodies interpreting them, thereby clarifying that music is a core necessity of her storytelling.

31. Bridgforth, *delta dandi,* 222.

32. Bridgforth, *delta dandi,* 222.

33. Richardson, *Queer Limit of Black Memory,* 185.

34. Royster, "Queering the Jazz Aesthetic," 550.

35. In quotations from Bridgforth's texts, slashes are as presented in the original. Slashes do not represent lines breaks in these instances.

The theatrical jazz text, therefore, is meant to be unpacked by the reader/witness, who must adjust their senses to the language and music of the novel in order to hear bull-jean's story.

Butch Realness: Flaws and All

Presented as mini chapters or episodes, the novel follows the adult life of bull-jean, a Black butch lesbian "everywoman" who, in living her life out of the closet in a rural town in Louisiana in the early twentieth century, represents the ups and downs of Black butch lesbian homemaking at the center of town (rather than the outskirts). Love is central to bull-jean's character, as she is in search of a femme lover that will "stay." Unlike in *A Lady and a Woman,* there is a section of town in *the bull-jean stories* where the queer and curious are able to socialize, date, and even perform in a local club in which blues music is the popular sonic backdrop of the day. A sanctuary for queer folk, the club is a haven that allows them to express themselves through walk, talk, and dress in nonnormative ways within a conservative community that tolerates its queer neighbors with fewer conditions than one without a queer subsect. The town's conditions, therefore, are less of a concern for the Black queer heroine of this story; she has her tribe. Instead, the noble butch's imperfections stand out as problems in need of solutions.

In twentieth-century media representations of masculine lesbians, the butch's flaws include misogyny, dominance, and aggression. In *The Witch's Flight,* Kara Keeling investigates the representation of the Black butch in the 1996 film *Set It Off.* Keeling unpacks Queen Latifah's memorably tough, cornrow-wearing, gun-wielding character, Cleo, as "a receptacle for the embattled, outlawed, and virulently heterosexual articulations of Black masculinity that undergird ghettocentrism."[36] She observes, "Cleo carries the weight of black masculinity so that the film's other perceptibly female characters, Stony, Frankie, and Tisean, can be recognized as 'ladies.'"[37] Keeling, here, identifies a certain necessity for masculinity in this woman-centered cops-and-robbers film in which a combination of financial insecurity, resentment, and greed lead Cleo and her friends to rob banks. While bull-jean is not a bank robber, there are similarities between her and Cleo, such as their stalwart devotion to their sister-friends, their sexual desire for women, and their masculine dress and behaviors. bull-jean's penchant for sentimentality and emotionality (she

36. Keeling, *Witch's Flight,* 124.
37. Keeling, *Witch's Flight,* 124.

is in love with the idea of love) is a difference. I do not mean to imply that butch lesbian characters in media do not have emotional attachments but, considering Keeling's reading, Cleo's role is the sturdy stud figure who does not break until she can no longer suppress her emotions. When depicted at all, Black female masculinity is often presented in the form of hypermasculine characters whose anger, violence, and lawlessness lead to tragedy.[38] Cleo's violent demise epitomizes this.

It is also interesting that the femme lesbian, Ursula, in *Set It Off* does not speak, an observation that Keeling highlights. Played by Samantha MacLachlan, Cleo's lively, blonde-haired, feminine girlfriend performs in absolute silence and is thereby reduced to an object of desire whose role is to pleasure Cleo with sensual lap dances. With that, Cleo is signified as "the man" in the relationship. Lesbian sexuality and sensuality are not problematic here; it is the lack of a femme lesbian point of view that assures their relationship is one-sided. Cleo's masculinity places Ursula in a position of power, but only by association. If Keeling is right and Cleo is a stand-in for Black masculinity, then her dominant positionality obscures the silent femme, pushing her aside to privilege the voice of her man-woman. Ursula's feminine body is on display as desirous and sexually arousing to her lover, but her body says little about her inner life. Essentially, without Cleo, she is merely flesh, blood, and bone; she is only a body without her voice. While bodies make meaning in motion, what Ursula has to say (her point of view) is held in Cleo's gaze; the femme is animated through the eyes of the butch. Once Cleo is killed by law enforcement at the end of the film, the femme fades away in the imagination of the viewers. Everybody remembers Cleo, but no one remembers Ursula.

The power dynamics between the butch and the femme are not as imbalanced in *the bull-jean stories*—the femme eventually talks back—but there is an imbalance until the femme demands parity. Bridgforth's depiction of this kind of power difference is a critique of the notion that hypermasculinity and butchness are synonymous, a performance that she saw play out in her family and community of origin. She writes:

> i saw myself more like those butch men than the femmes that raised me/but i did not like the way the men underestimated talked down to and mistreated the femmes. i understood that the very conservative south they had all fled from/was present somehow within the confines of the female-male games they played.[39]

38. Another example of a representation of the Black lesbian gangster with a heart of gold is Snoop (played by Felicia "Snoop" Pearson) in the television series *The Wire* (2002–8).

39. Bridgforth, "a wo'mn called sir," 46.

The "female-male games" that the butches and femmes play in *bull-jean* are essentially that—*play*. As such, the rules of the games can change to suit the needs of the Black queer women at the center of the narrative. Clearly, Bridgforth is playing with gender in her work to explore the gender dynamics between characters of the same biological sex. In doing so, she declares that hypermasculinity is an inauthentic performance that, if left unchecked, can pose limitations to the comfort of masculine and feminine same-gender-loving women.

With bull-jean, Bridgforth complicates the butch stereotype and extends the boundaries of what a butch can be and do in performance. The depiction of bull-jean as a masculine woman with feminine behaviors transforms viewers' perceptions of the butch. When they think they can put bull-jean in a recognizably butch box, that vision is disrupted to reveal the smooth edges of her personality. There are moments of identification when audiences see beyond her butchness. For example, while the narrators (bull-jean's mostly masculine women kin) decry her pitiful state (begging, pleading, reciting poetry and "croon'n" outside of her lovers' windows), the audience is compelled to identify with the sympathetic figure as a woman longing for a lover.

Love also leaves bull-jean in emotional anguish. There is something sad and humorous about her inability to keep a lover considering the depths of her acts of lovin' on others; the repetition of loss and the narrators' "reads" of bull-jean and her women are exceedingly funny as they reveal bull-jean's habitual enmeshment with the subjects of her desire. When a relationship fails, she falls into a deep depression, and her real-life blues carries over into her nightlife as a male impersonator who sings the blues in the local juke joint. Making connections between blues, jazz, and sexual freedom, Omi Osun Joni L. Jones claims, "It is no surprise that Bridgforth's jazz rests deep inside its blues roots given the abundance of sexually transgressive women she creates."[40] The narrators—although quick to quip about bull-jean's relationships—want to help her and regularly offer advice she rarely takes. As griots themselves, many of the narrators have similar stories to tell. For instance, bugga, a lesbian who "counsel[s] wid" bull-jean, has made similar missteps in love and disregarded the advice of older, wiser women. This recognition prompts bugga to tell bull-jean to "*RUN!!!*" if she "*feels anythang what resemble Lovve,*"[41] but bull-jean has romanticized love to the extent that she expects it to hurt, and lovin' (outside of the pleasure-pain of erotic acts) should not cause pain.

40. O. Jones, *Theatrical Jazz*, 124.

41. Bridgforth, *bull-jean stories*, 34–37. Further references to this work are cited parenthetically.

While bull-jean's experiences of loss occur primarily in her romantic life, a more significant loss haunts her past. Her son (son-man) was taken away from her by authorities who judged her unfit to be a mother because of her identity. Her nonnormative gender expression and sexuality violated the community's politics of respectability, and action was taken to remove the child from her home. As a result, bull-jean is in a revolving love-loss-grief loop in her romantic life. When son-man returns, it becomes clear that she has been trapped in this painful cycle because motherhood was an important part of her identity and, as long as she and her child are separated, she will struggle to hold on to any kind of domestic love.

Although bull-jean experiences considerable emotional pain, she also experiences considerable pleasure in the club space. In *Get Yo' Life: Black Queer Placemaking,* R. J. Millhouse writes, "Black LGBTQ club spaces, for example, are not fixed; they are produced by communal performance and interior interactions within club spaces, including dance, interpersonal interactions, symbolic objects, and sonic rhythms."[42] Normalizing queerness in the Black South, the club becomes an important social space for the characters in *bull-jean* to congregate and perform in subversive ways that, as Millhouse shows in his study of the Black queer club, "may heal and affirm them."[43] Ironically, straight and queer worlds collide in Club Seeyaround, a private space to which folks come to relax from the pressures of heteronormativity and Black respectability. The popular hangout is one of the joints in which bull-jean lounges and croons as b.j. la rue. Of gender bending and the centrality of the club, Bridgforth writes, "In them juke joints, they was doin' everything, and they didn't have the hang-ups that we have today."[44] The club, as she sees it, has been a space of freedom where alternative performances of gender and sexuality are acceptable. Of the rent parties in 1920s Harlem—similar to the weekend parties at Southern juke joints—James F. Wilson observes that "the admixture of alcohol, jazz music, and feelings of political and social liberation engendered at these parties contributed to a sense of sexual freedom as well."[45] Similarly, Ramón H. Rivera-Servera finds that the contemporary club can be a freeing space where queers of color practice "choreographies of resistance"—"embodied practices through which [they as] minoritarian subjects claim their space in social and cultural realms."[46] Such

42. Millhouse, *Get Yo' Life,* 2.

43. Millhouse, *Get Yo' Life,* 3.

44. González, "Interview with Sharon Bridgforth," 231.

45. Wilson, *Bulldaggers, Pansies, and Chocolate Babies,* 19. The popular music at Club Seeyaround is blues, an appropriate style for the melancholy bull-jean.

46. Rivera-Servera, *Performing Queer Latinidad,* 161.

FIGURE 3. Aimee K. Bryant as bull-jean in *the bull-jean stories.* Pillsbury House + Theatre, 2024. Photograph by Bruce Silcox.

choreographies arise from communal engagement in pleasure-making (singing, dancing, partying, drinking, smoking, loving) in the club.

bull-jean performs her own brand of masculinity at Club Seeyaround and other nonqueer clubs in town in convincing drag (see figure 3). Claiming the stage as b.j. enables her to make the club home for the night, no matter the clientele. She/he/they affirm their right to be there and is supported by others (straight and queer) in that effort. In the scene titled "bull-jean is b.j. la rue," the narrator divulges that she thought bull-jean *was* a man by her appearance and behavior on stage. When she heard b.j. sing, she was reminded of tootie la rue, bull-jean's father, which suggests that bull-jean may be affecting her father's singing voice to appear more authentic (64). The narrator explains,

> parently the club owners twist off she name
> make more money letting the mens think
> her a man-sangn-man-sorrows. (66–67)

Not only can bull-jean pass for a man in the club, but drag performance is lucrative in other ways. A wanderer, bull-jean is able to move in and out of queer and straight worlds with flexibility and privilege. According to Judith Butler, "There are advantages to remaining less than intelligible. . . . Indeed, if my options are loathsome, if I have no desire to be recognized within a certain set of norms, then it follows that my sense of survival depends upon escaping the clutch of those norms by which recognition is conferred."[47] From a heterocentric viewpoint, bull-jean is masculine (or "like a man") and is, therefore, not wholly legible as either gender. When she is b.j., however, bull-jean is unrecognizable as a woman to cisgender men. b.j. is not a disguise, to be sure, but he provides a layer of protection for bull-jean.

To further complicate things, bull-jean's intersectional identity also includes the role of mother. In "Butches with Babies: Reconfiguring Gender and Motherhood," Rachel Epstein observes that "butch motherhood itself is not a new phenomenon."[48] Tracing butch motherhood back to the 1940s and 1950s, she notes that, historically, butch lesbians have received pushback from heterosexuals and lesbians for choosing motherhood. She writes: "Butch mothers perform the unexpected in many directions. Butches are not supposed to be mothers, and mothers are not supposed to be butch. When butches mother they denaturalize both terms and transform both subjectivities."[49] bull-jean embraced her role as mother, but she experienced, firsthand, the ability of those in positions of power to judge her unfit to mother because she is a lesbian. bull-jean's and her son's experience with state authorities illuminates a probable consequence of mothering as a queer person in a homophobic society.

bull-jean & the women

bull-jean's gender play on stage also finds its way into her home as she navigates the hills and valleys of romances with women who, mostly, leave her. Her many lovers—the wo'mn, babett, clara, sugga, safirra, and serafine—are basically the same woman—a bicurious cisgender femme experimenting with lesbianism. The femmes may give bull-jean "everthang," but they take her lovin' and run (86). Also, they rarely speak, as their actions and motives are relayed to the reader/audience by the butch-griot-narrator-friends of bull-jean. The femmes are generally considered manipulative straddlers unsure of embarking on a long-lasting relationship with a woman or a man; however, neither bisexual identity nor sexual fluidity are considered in the narrators' assessments of the femmes' queerness. In *Sexual Fluidity: Understanding Women's Love and Desire,* Lisa M. Diamond explains, "[Sexual fluidity] means

47. Butler, *Undoing Gender,* 3.
48. Epstein, "Butches with Babies," 44.
49. Epstein, "Butches with Babies," 55.

situation-dependent flexibility in women's sexual responsiveness. This flexibility makes it possible for some women to experience desires for either men or women under certain circumstances, regardless of their overall sexual orientation."[50] Many of the femmes in *bull-jean* appear sexually fluid and, as such, may experience moments of indecision or confusion around their sexuality. They may also be afraid or ashamed of their queer desire and, instead of parading around town with bull-jean, choose to have their dalliances with her in private, while keeping a "straight" face in public.

Inconsiderate of the delicate nature of coming out in the South safely, the butch narrators take the position that a "good" femme is hard to find. For example, safirra goode is described as "two-sided/walk ever whicha way/lik she gots to have it all   mens in the street/bull-jean in the sheets/jes all-of-it" (45). The narrator polices safirra's queer experimentation and scrutinizes her for not performing queerness "properly"; however, bull-jean's romantic and sexual behaviors do not check the boxes of the narrator's queer ethics either. When bull-jean plays the field, it is acceptable, but when safirra plays the field, her actions are deemed condemnable. Boxed in between heteronormativity and homonormativity, *no wonder she don't talk.* In another scene, bull-jean and jucey la bloom sit drinking and crying over a character called the wo'mn. The wo'mn has broken bull-jean's heart. According to the narrator,

> jucey say
> *she ain't nuthn but a periodic-ho   ain't even got sense nuff*
> *to charge on a regular basis.* (24)

This dig at the wo'mn reflects jucey and bull-jean's butch bond—"they so close they feel one-the-other's pain"—and with it comes a contemptuous utterance bordering on misogynoir (23). Moreover, bull-jean continuously falls for emotionally unavailable yet physically desirable women. Objectifying the femmes, she is misled by superficial factors (such as the wo'mn's voluptuous physique and sexual stride) that, to her, are features of an ideal partner. Referring to her as "trouble" and "it," while conversing with jucey, the wo'mn is reduced to both object and subject of bull-jean's desire. *No wonder she don't stay.*

The temporal concept of "last-Life" is significant to bull-jean's struggles in love in *this* life. If her "last-Life" failings dictate the quality of her current relationships, then, consistent with this spiritual logic, bull-jean never had a chance with any woman. Spirituality, religion, and love converge in "bull-jean

---

50. Diamond, *Sexual Fluidity*, 3.

& next life/blues"—a scene in which the audience learns about bull-jean's relationship with safirra goode—a preacher's daughter—and safirra's arranged marriage to sampson tucka johnson—a preacher's son. The omniscient narrator characterizes safirra and sampson as incorrigibles whose fathers (the reverends) have arranged a marriage between the two to force them to settle down. Acquiescing, they agree to marry in a church ceremony. The problem is that safirra is also dating bull-jean. Per the narrator, the community is fully aware that she is "bull-jean's wo'mn!" (44). In a compulsory move to "play" straight, safirra must marry a man. She even convinces bull-jean to attend and witness "the most important event in [her] life" (as if bull-jean were only a friend) (45–46). She agrees to witness the ceremony, but being the hero of this story, she cannot sit idly by as her lover marries someone else. When the preacher asks if anyone in the congregation objects to the marriage, bull-jean stands up in the middle of the ceremony and professes her love for safirra. Objecting to the marriage, bull-jean steals focus. To her, safirra and tucka's union is an illegitimate "binding."

The congregation becomes silent, mostly, but some of the onlookers laugh. When conchita la fraud and wee wee "[giggle] in the back of the church," they are cackling not only at bull-jean, but about the entire spectacle (51). They are aware that she and safirra were lovers and that bull-jean has been humiliated by the engagement. They also know, per the community's unspoken politics of respectability, that bull-jean does not have the support or authority to contest the marriage. This dual response from the congregation—silence and laughter—arises for several reasons, one of which is that bull-jean is a female dressed in men's formal wear, an uncommon sight for this time. Again, she is unintelligible as a man outside of the club and does not adhere to the community's conceptualization of a "proper" man or woman. Even though she is comfortable in her suit, the attendees are not comfortable with her wearing it. bull-jean's clothing also suggests that she is prepared to step into the groom's place, if safirra will have her.

Her vision of a queer marriage in a conservative time and space is incomprehensible to a congregation prepared to witness a heterosexual marriage, and while they believe bull-jean should be ashamed of herself, she believes that safirra, tucka, and the reverends are the shameful ones because they are perpetuating a lie. bull-jean was reared in the church and is familiar with the underlying meanings of the institution's religious traditions and practices. Similar to Flora in *A Lady and a Woman,* bull-jean adheres to a Christian value system in which lying is sinful and loving is not. She literally stands up for what she believes—representing all queer folk—and claims the sacred in "this life" so as to lay the spiritual groundwork for the next.

The Femme's Speech / son-man's Return

mina is bull-jean's last attempt at love. In "bull-jean & mina stay," bull-jean asks mina to be her wife, but, instead of joy, the proposal incites a tense exchange. The narrator, an unnamed relative of mina, briefly summarizes their family history of resisting authority, an important characteristic that informs mina's actions and utterances. When mina questions bull-jean's reason for proposing, she speaks for women who have barely survived patriarchal control. She is concerned that if she commits to bull-jean as a bride to a groom, bull-jean will dominate her as her ex-husband did. Therefore, mina verbalizes her disinterest in being anyone's traditional wife. It seems that bull-jean's masculinist treatment of mina is the source of their difficulty in speaking across the butch-femme divide. This confrontation is a pivotal moment of crisis. The narrator advises:

> bull-jean want mina stay mus talk no-bark no act-out
> cause mina see a barkn dog/move on
> bull-jean cain't capture mina/mina got ta want come
> stay. (87)

bull-jean must soften if she wants mina to stay. She must also find the "right" word(s) because, as the narrator notes, "wife ain't saying nuthn right/in [mina's] mind!" mina associates the word "wife" with bad feelings, preferring the more autonomous "wo'mn" (88). mina's feminist and femme-centric world has no room for bull-jean's unbalanced approach to lovin' on her. In this context, there is a negative potential of lovin' on when the lovers' intent stems from fear of losing the other. bull-jean's personal losses have led her to love women from a place of fear, which cheapens her lovin' acts. mina recognizes this version as a knockoff of the "real thing"—a simulacrum in the Baudrillardian sense.

Watching the scene unfold, the narrator stands nervously on her porch, enthralled by the dramatic conflict, and wondering how bull-jean will respond to mina's provocation. Breaking a lengthy silence, she reproposes to mina, painting the moment with poetry that is, at once, holy and romantic. By invoking spirituality and corporeality, bull-jean allows both concepts to meld into one, forming the basis from which she will better care for her wo'mn. Affirming mina's voice, bull-jean replies:

> **i want you to**
> **stay**

> **be who you are wid fierceness**
> **be honest wid me**
> **and see me when you look**
> **that is what i want/that's**
> **what i am asking   be**
> **my wo'mn mina.** (91)

To ask mina to *see* her is to suggest that the persona bull-jean presents to the outside world is an incomplete portrait. mina's acceptance of the new proposal, therefore, brings an end to a butch-femme reckoning that precedes the most healing lovin' on she experiences in the novel.

A neighbor, pontificuss "cuss" devine johnson, narrates the final episode, "bull-jean & the question of family." Since marrying, the couple are now mothers to numerous children who regularly disrupt cuss's peace and quiet. She explains that the children are not all biological—

> some is theys/some is nieces nephews
> neighbors and cousins. (99–100)

The family is not complete, however, until bull-jean's adult child, son-man, returns. pontificuss reports that son-man arrived on the couple's porch one Saturday with his adopted son. In the emotional retelling of this happening, the dialogue shifts from third person (cuss) to first person (son-man) and back to third person (cuss). His life has been turbulent, as evidenced by his scarred face and hands. mina sees him first, then calls bull-jean to the porch. Clearly, bull-jean has talked about him because this is the first time mina and son-man meet, yet "[she] know him right off." To be expected, bull-jean is stunned by his presence and cannot find words to speak to him, but son-man, who has waited many years to see her again, delivers a lengthy heart-wrenching monologue detailing his painful sojourn. Sitting at his mother's feet, son-man describes being taken from her arms as a boy and being forced into those of a new family in which religion was used as a corrective tool and a way to replace the image he had of a lovin' mother with the image of an "*unholy*" one—"*a sinner gonn burn in hell*" (103). It is also revealed that he was forbidden to search for her, under threat that she would be jailed.

son-man admits that being separated from bull-jean left him with an unstable foundation. He asserts that she taught him how to be a man, rejecting the pervasive rhetoric that women cannot raise men—that is, there must be a male figure in the home for boys to acquire the "right" racialized and gendered lessons and life skills. From son-man's point of view, bull-jean raised him well, and he has longed for her mothering since he was taken from her. They both share the trauma of loss, by virtue of him being ripped from her arms. In this mother-son story, son-man's liberation from the residual effects of trauma is indivisibly linked to hers. The narrator observes bull-jean's response to his celebration of her parenting: "she couldn't talk for a long time/just sit hold the hands of her manchild/crying out the left side she face smiling" (108). The past and future meet in the present as the butch mother reconciles both her greatest love and even greater loss.

In *the bull-jean stories,* bull-jean is in active pursuit of joy within and without a community whose embrace is conditional. Way out of the closet, she is encouraged to be discreet about her sexual liaisons, engaging in a dance with herself and her communities that is seemingly at odds, the result of which is a tired two-step in public and a rousing Black Bottom shimmy in private. Dancing between cultures, bull-jean embodies a male alter ego in the queer nightclub space that allows her to act out and into a world of her own. The religious and spiritual violence she has experienced—most notably losing her son to the state and being silenced by the church—force bull-jean to rely heavily on her alter ego to maintain power and control in a community in which, as a woman and a lesbian, she has little. In the club space, b.j. la rue is a diplomatic persona and a more freeing butch embodiment, but when b.j. makes his way into bull-jean's personal life, the hypermasculinity of that performance complicates her homemaking.

bull-jean's transformation by and through lovin' without conditions or pretense is spearheaded by a butch fantasy captured in a femme reality. The fantastic and the real find their groove in this novel as the butch and femme cleave together in an alliance that extends and bolsters their family unit. Fantasy, Jill Dolan argues, "offers the potential for changing gender-coded structures of power."[51] Fantasy, here, should not be taken as unrealistic but as larger than life, and it enables bull-jean to disidentify with institutions that consider her unrespectable. As she moves in and out of love with various femmes, the butch fantasy she conjures in the club empowers her in ways that become useful on the outside. With mina's help (her femme reality), bull-jean is thrust into consciousness, so to speak, drawing a line between fantasy and reality to achieve the romance she desperately wants. Her misplacement of love for her lost child onto women who cannot possibly fill that void almost always leads to abandonment, but mina's feminist ultimatum is a wakeup call for bull-jean to love her in a different way—not obsessively but mutually—which is a shift that enables bull-jean to relax her tough exterior and prepares her to receive

---

51. Dolan, *Feminist Spectator as Critic,* 68.

her son—the missing piece of her life that had been replaced by memories too traumatic to revisit.

My grandfather taught me that when memories are all we have left, storytelling can cement them in those who live on without us—rooting memory in time that is cyclical wherein birth, life, and death comingle. In life, he held our family's wayward parts together, reminding us that we had a deep foundation from which to live our chosen lives. In death, he remains our patriarch and our keeper of stories. He was proudly rooted in Georgia, a state he unequivocally called home despite his ancestors being enslaved and forced to work the land, and despite the large and small humiliations he experienced as a Black person in the South. Georgia is where he made community. It is where he raised his children and grandchildren. It is where he planted the hopes and dreams he kept largely to himself. If a Black man could make a home, raise a family, and contribute to community in the rural South in a time of unbelievable opposition to Black personhood, comfort, and survival, then it is not speculative to imagine that a Black lesbian man-woman like bull-jean could too.

CHAPTER 3

Girls Like Her

Butch Girlhood and the Black Family in *the cowboy is dying* and *Pariah*

On the night of May 11, 2003, fifteen-year-old Sakia Gunn, a few friends, and a cousin were returning to Newark, New Jersey, from Christopher Street Pier in Greenwich Village—a popular gathering spot for queer and transgender youth commonly referred to as "The Pier."[1] The minor girls, waiting for a bus that would take them home, were approached by two men in a car who propositioned them sexually. Sakia responded, as did the others, by telling them no. Angered by the response or by how they said it, the men exited the car. One of them—a large, Black man with neat locs in his thirties named Robert McCullough, who, in court footage, looks like the harmless unofficial uncle at the neighborhood barbecue—responded to Sakia by putting a knife to her throat.[2] Perhaps, by intimidating her, he thought she would apologize or recoil with an "I'm sorry" or "I'm good. I've got a boyfriend." Or, maybe he clocked her queerness straight away and intended to make a point to the girls dressed in masculine street clothes, and passersby, that no matter how boyish they were, as females, they were powerless. Or, perhaps he figured that if she wanted to act like a man, he would treat her like one. It seems that his fragile masculinity required him to perform his gender in such a violent way to prove to his ride-along buddy that he was a "real" man. A senseless crime fueled by

1. To learn more about the queer history of The Pier, see Bratton's *Pier Kids*.
2. See Brack, *Dreams Deferred*.

homophobia, this attack was a message to *girls like her*—the girls who wear short brush cuts and baggy clothes, the girls who dare to love on other girls, and girls who talk back when men sexually harass them.

As he towered over her, she did not deny her queer identity; in fact, those who bore witness maintain that she doubled down on it. Belinda Deneen Wallace and Tanya L. Shields rightly state, "Claiming Black queerness [can] mean negotiating homophobic pain and trauma. Sometimes the damage inflicted by communities is explicit, such as ostracism; at other times, these harms are implicit, such as the expectation that queer people keep silent."[3] Both harms were inflicted upon Sakia that night. As her cousin, Valencia Bailey, testified in court, Sakia's "no" should have marked the end of the interaction; it did not. Enraged by the presence of a butch girl and her tribe, most of whom identified as AGs, or aggressive lesbians, McCullough stabbed her in the chest then drove away. Sakia later died in her cousin's arms in the parking lot of a local hospital. To him, a mouthy Black butch girl was an abnormal girl exhibiting intolerable female excesses: outspokenness, agency, and confidence. In his inability to see her humanity, to see her as part of an extended family to which they both belonged, he denied her a loving future.

The early plays of Donnetta Lavinia Grays and films of Dee Rees attend to the challenges of Black queer girls transitioning to womanhood while navigating biological and queer families that often misrecognize them and attempt to shape them into the kind of women they deem respectable. In this chapter, I focus on Grays's and Rees's early productions, *the cowboy is dying* (2008) and *Pariah* (2011), respectively, both of which are narratives that center Black queer girls in search of unconditional familial ties in Southern and Northern contexts. These works directly respond to the violences—physical, spiritual, and emotional—that befall queer girls coming of age in Black communities, which, to be clear, are largely conservative and therefore suspicious and critical of signs of queerness, especially in children. Grays's and Rees's depictions of butch girlhood elucidate the complexities of embodying "acceptable" performances of masculinity for the queer child navigating the respectability politics of Black queer and Black straight spaces.

Black women artists' first works tend to present rough sketches of familiar people and cultural situations, capturing raw truths and desires that stem from lived experiences; *the cowboy is dying* and *Pariah* are no different. Most significantly, they nod to Black queer futures that Grays and Rees could have only imagined for themselves as young lesbians raised in the South. Considering a history of violence toward Black queer girls, such as the senseless murder

3. Wallace and Shields, "Introduction: Quotidian Futures," 105.

of Sakia Gunn, both works chronicle the paths of two girls—Donnetta and Alike—who yearn to be loved on, and who rely on literary and performing arts as outlets to articulate their present conditions and reimagine a world wherein girls like them can live longer and prouder.

In *Charting the Afrofuturist Imaginary in African American Arts* (2023), Elizabeth Carmel Hamilton writes, "Afrofuturist artists have an orientation toward what is to come while being constantly aware of the past. They have expansive imaginations, expanding on what is possible, not just what the world has offered in the past. They are creatively innovating with concepts and images."[4] While Afrofuturism can materialize in literature, theater, and film as psychedelic, otherworldly illustrations wherein machines, time-travelers, and artificial intelligence are characters, as in the science fiction novels of Octavia E. Butler, Afrofuturism can also be semi-surreal coming-out-while-coming-of-age stories highlighting the dialectics of straight mother–queer daughter relationships, butch embodiment, first love, and the healing power of future-affirming art on the Black queer psyche.

While the aesthetic, technical, and practical necessities of playmaking and filmmaking differ greatly, there are character and narrative commonalities between Grays's play and Rees's film that invite comparison. Both center on protagonists and plotlines that represent aspects of the lived experiences of their creators. Second, each protagonist finds herself actively maneuvering through the labyrinth of adolescence toward adulthood by altering language and embodiment to "fit" into multiple communities, the result of which is a disingenuous performance of self that begs correction, or, better, alteration. Grays and Rees shine a light on masculine-of-center girls who reach adulthood without having to deny their romantic and sexual desires for those of the same gender. Third, although set in different regions of the United States, both characters choose to leave "home" for environments that afford them the freedom to pursue love openly; form a tribe of like-minded friends; and develop intellectual perspectives independent of their parents.

the cowboy is dying

Actress and playwright Donnetta Lavinia Grays has received numerous honors for her writing including the Whiting Award for Drama and the Helen Merrill Award for Playwriting. Grays has balanced a vast stage and screen acting and writing career since the early 2000s. Her plays have been produced at

4. Hamilton, *Charting the Afrofuturist Imaginary*, 3.

Steppenwolf, Denver Center for the Performing Arts, Alabama Shakespeare Festival, Dallas Theater Center, and WP Theater. Grays's early works were produced in nonqueer, commercial theaters that invested in her early solo work, including Coyote REP Theatre Company, which commissioned her 2008 solo play *the cowboy is dying.*[5] Inspired by Sharon Bridgforth's novel, Grays admits, "reading [*the bull-jean stories*] gave me permission to write because I saw [someone] like me in her and her words."[6]

In this semi-autobiographical production, Grays embodies nineteen characters including her adolescent, teenage, and adult selves, and a lesbian cowboy named Bulldagger. Grays reproduces the butch archetype then dismantles it (as hinted in the play's title) through an imaginative solo performance that combines theatrical styles and aesthetics, including musical theater, to document Donnetta's Black queer migration. *cowboy* follows Donnetta's maturation from eight years old to thirty years old and is set in multiple locations—Columbia and Charleston, South Carolina, and Brooklyn, New York. The minimalist play can be designed in creative ways that allude to these cities without the use of "any large set pieces" to represent them.[7] The stage is split; there is an empty playing space on one side "where Donnetta lives" and an apartment on the other side "where Bulldagger lives" (2). While the characters inhabit different playing spaces, they share realistic psychological worlds. That is, although Bulldagger is a fantastical alter ego that young Donnetta shapes in her imagination, the playwright notes that the cowboy is "not otherworldly"; she lives in her own reality. And as the play unfolds, both worlds (Donnetta's and Bulldagger's) begin to merge (2).

Bulldagger is a masculine character who dresses in cowboy attire; she is a striking presence whom Grays describes as "solid and strong, but embattled" (3). Like bull-jean, she is a lover of love and has her heart set on marrying her girlfriend (named "The lover"). The lover—who is never embodied, only spoken of—is a femme ideal in Bulldagger's world, although the relationship, it is revealed, is turbulent at times. The play's opening scene takes place outside of Bulldagger's apartment as she prepares to propose marriage to The lover. Bulldagger paces as she attempts to recite her proposal speech. Struggling to speak the words, she sings them in a folksy blues called "Feel Good." In the tradition of queer blues of the past, the lyrics of "Feel Good" focus squarely on the Lover's body and imply that Bulldagger worships it (3).[8] The song is

5. Coyote REP, now closed, was a nonprofit theater company that opened in 2006.

6. Author email correspondence with Grays, October 22, 2011.

7. Grays, *the cowboy is dying* (unpublished), 2. Further references to this source are cited parenthetically.

8. See Grays, "Make Me Feel Good," to hear an audio recording.

seductive rather than inductive, the latter of which one might expect of a proposal. However, for a cowboy, like her, the body is key—how it looks, how it feels, what it does. The external is of maximum importance to this masculine woman who defines herself by the strength of her body and its appearance. If she performs the proposal "right"—if she is sexy, macho, and sweet—then the lover will accept, thereby making her "feel good."

The erotic, in the Lordeian sense, explains the centrality of sex in Bulldagger's intoned proposal. In "Why We Get Off: Moving Towards a Black Feminist Politics of Pleasure," Joan Morgan disagrees with those who have made a distinction between Audre Lorde's oft-referenced concept of the erotic and physical sex. She writes, "Some black feminists have chosen to map a binary and heteronormative read onto Lorde's erotic that implies that the erotic can only be achieved by a transcendence of mere sex, or by eschewing sex that isn't relegated to the realms of romantic love or the spiritual."[9] Morgan encourages a sex-positive, sex-inclusive reading of Lorde's description of the "erotic" and its uses as a natural interpretation, considering Lorde's insistence upon the importance of her lesbian identity to her feminist politics. Morgan rightly calls out the exclusion of the sexual body from erotic discourse in Black feminist thought and vies for "an erotic that demands space be made for honest bodies that like to also *fuck*."[10] Thus, when Bulldagger speaks of wanting to feel "good," she means it, in every sense.

After the song, Bulldagger places her hat down on a table and transforms into adolescent Donnetta, who is seated "in the backyard of her parent's house in Columbia, South Carolina" (4). She explains, "Our backyard is so huge. I like to come out here barefoot so I can feel the thick blades of grass run between my toes. I center myself between the tiny weeping willow tree and the deck. And I am waiting for my rainstorm to arrive" (4). This tactile description indicates that the girl is present in her body; it also suggests that she is prepared, endowed with her own power to combat a storm that is not only a metaphor for life but for God Himself—neither of which she fears. At eight years old, Donnetta fearlessly takes control of "her" rainstorm, by claiming it. Her connection with nature relates directly to her faith in God and her ability to converse with Him as a playmate. A plucky child, she genuinely believes that she can control nature because she is "tight" with God; her gender, at this point, does not impact the hierarchy of that relationship. There is none, yet. She has what is often referred to in the Southern Black Christian church as

9. Morgan, "Why We Get Off," 34.
10. Morgan, "Why We Get Off," 34.

"a relationship with God." She speaks upward to heaven while a dark cloud moves in over the city, proclaiming:

> I am the shore. Wash your dark tide upon me great big ole dark storm cloud! Come on. Come on. I am a conductor of the thunder, a coddler of lightning. A sorcerer who calls down the rains in all their glorious frenzy. I am a challenger. I am . . . eight years old. And I have the balls to challenge God. (5)

Oblivious to the destructive potential of the storm/God, she dares it/Him to draw close.

The concepts of religion and the "after life" are important to Donnetta. Her family has recently changed churches, and although they are still influenced by their previous denomination (the Baptist Church), they are now, as she phrases it, "transitional Southern Baptist/semi-practicing Jehovah's Witness[es]" (10). Her bible study teacher has taught her that there are only 144,000 people on earth who are "truly saved," and only they "will be called upon to live in heaven and serve alongside God after Armageddon." Adhering to this fundamental precept, Donnetta wants to be in that number of saints (10). Through her conversations with God, she believes she has been "called" to the ministry—"God tells me . . . I got me a slot! He tells me that I am called to preach. He tells me that I am called into the ministry" (10). Donnetta's experience of hearing the "call" is an ecstatic revelation that poses a major obstacle for a girl whose homoerotic desires and boyish conduct are in stark opposition to the church's expectations of a preacher, let alone a female preacher.

In the South, two of the most beloved pastimes are sports and religion. Being active in religious circles entails attending church services, prayer meetings, bible study classes, and Sunday school—all of which are family- and community-centered activities. Many Black folks raised in the church environment fondly associate their childhoods with these social events and the messages communicated there by religious leaders. For fundamentalists, homosexuality is generally considered a sin, and that sentiment, historically, has been preached from pulpits with the expectation that the congregation agrees. The church is not a space in which the *word* (God's directive), as interpreted by theologians and preachers (often male), is challenged outright. If one disagrees, they find another church, but rarely do they talk back to God's interlocutors. Donnetta's internal conflict is rooted in a fear of sinning—in thought and act—and, thereby, becoming unfit to preach. With that, she suppresses her queer fantasies as a "good" church girl is wont to do.

FIGURE 4. Donnetta Lavinia Grays in *the cowboy is dying*. Coyote REP Theatre Company, 2008. Photograph by Deidre Schoo.

Feminist theorists, like Judith Lorber, have argued that gender, as a social construct, is learned, and children are taught the behavioral expectations associated with being a boy or a girl and reproduce it in their own lives.[11] Those expectations exclude homosexuality. This belief system (in Donnetta's realistic world) informs Bulldagger's performance of masculinity (in her surrealistic world)—one that is curiously similar to the cool, dangerous cowboy type made famous by Clint Eastwood in Sergio Leone westerns such as *The Outlaw Josey Wales* (see figure 4). However, in the "real" world, Donnetta is still a child, and, as such, she plays within the confines of the tomboy type. As she ages, the stakes of playing with gender heighten. For preteens and teenagers exploring masculinity in girlhood, the identity of tomboy emerges as a natural, yet temporary state of being.

Some boyish girls identify (or are labeled by others) as tomboys based on their behaviors (such as playing sports, doing outdoor activities, wearing boyish clothes and playing with toys traditionally assigned to boys). Jack Halberstam defines "tomboyism" as "generally describ[ing] an extended childhood period of female masculinity," thereby suggesting that there is a cut-off for this identity and its associated behaviors for girls.[12] In "Tomboy as a Protective

11. See Lorber, "Night to His Day."
12. Halberstam, *Female Masculinity*, 5.

Identity," Traci Craig and Jessica LaCroix argue that "tomboy as used by specific populations provides groups of girls/women with limited protections" including "(1) sexual reputation protection for heterosexual girls and women; (2) protection for lesbians who are closeted; and (3) protected access to male privileged spaces, activities, and conversations."[13] These protections are necessary at this age, before one's sexual identity is made public or recognized by the girl child or adolescent, and allows them to play in nonnormative ways, or the ways in which a "good girl" is expected to perform in girlhood.

For biological females, tomboyism can provide a welcome label that shields them until they figure out who they are in terms of gender and sexuality. It can be a placeholder for their developing identities in a heterosexist world. Betsy Levonian Morgan observes, "Although childhood tomboy behavior appears to have benefits throughout life, tomboyism appears to abate around puberty when girls experience increasing social pressure to act in gender appropriate ways."[14] Morgan's study of "three generations of women's self-perceptions of tomboyism" characterizes tomboy behavior as a normal part of girls' development and finds that nearly 50 percent of girls enact some form of tomboy behavior. She argues that tomboyism—be it a phase in girlhood or adopted as a long-term identity—helps girls become independent and comfortable asserting themselves.[15] Regarding the tolerance of tomboy behavior, Halberstam says that most parents allow their female children to act out this behavior up to a certain age, whereas boys who act out feminine behavior are immediately and forcefully redirected. Furthermore, Halberstam says, "If we are to believe general accounts of childhood behavior, tomboyism is quite common for girls and does not generally give rise to parental fears. Girls are more often expected to conform to a more feminine normative than boys are, which can result in confusion and isolation."[16] Therefore, Donnetta's tomboyism obscures her queerness in her adolescent years, but, as she becomes a young adult, acting upon her romantic and sexual desires, and performing her ideal gendered self, uncovers a dual queerness that religion cannot undo.

Northern Exposure

After high school, Donnetta moves to New York City to pursue an acting career. In the process of this transition, she gains fifteen pounds of muscle

13. Craig and LaCroix, "Tomboy as a Protective Identity," 450.
14. Morgan, "Three Generational Study," 790.
15. Morgan, "Three Generational Study," 785.
16. Halberstam, *Female Masculinity*, 5.

mass and cuts her hair into a cropped Afro hairstyle. She is stronger, more liberated, and on a path to becoming a working artist—"I'm kind of a stud. The cowboy of my youth. Quiet. Not brooding yet, mysterious. A seriously intense lover of great dimension" (19–20). The life changes she has made, including ending her relationship with her first and last boyfriend Ed and moving away from home, have led her to affirm herself as the "stud" (like Bulldagger) she always dreamed of becoming. It is intimated that moving north is the only option for her, although her love for the South never dissipates. For queer youth raised in the South, the region can become less safe as they mature, especially if they self-identify as queer and desire to be transparent about it. While Donnetta essentially migrates north for a better life, she finds that, even there, making the urban space home does not come easily to her as a Southern girl. It requires effort to fit into the liberal, bustling culture and to find a community of friends that embraces all of her identities.

Initially a friend, Stacey becomes her first lover. They have a one-night stand—a rite of passage for the young lesbian—and, afterward, Donnetta buys a new pair of boots. As a masculine-of-center woman, she presents a version of herself she thinks her partners want, thereby stunting her growth as an individual. Because she has developed a structured identity based on reproduced images and narratives of rigid performances of masculinity, it is difficult for her to color outside of those lines and create an identity that envelops her femininity, masculinity, vulnerability, and insecurities.

> After Stacey, my problem isn't bringing women into my life or making love to them for that matter. I mean I'm no lady killer or anything but, I begin to present my heart as a home of sorts and they respond by looking down at my feet and seeing what they believe to be a grounded pair of size nines, that my frame is sturdy and that maybe, just maybe . . . a cowboy's finally come to their rescue. (22)

This last statement may or may not be true, hence the use of the word "maybe." The butch perspective, if unchecked, can overshadow the femme, muddying the coexisting truths of the narrative forwarded by the butch. The femmes Donnetta refers to do not speak for themselves, thereby limiting what can be known about the totality of her relationships with them. The important information in this commentary is how Donnetta views herself. She does not believe that she is the cowboy, yet; she is not bulky enough, her feet are not big enough, and she is not imposing enough to play the cowboy convincingly. While it is unclear how becoming the Bulldagger will serve Donnetta in the long run, it is an ideal that has meaning for her in the here and now, just as forming a diverse, supportive circle of queer womenkin in her new city is.

She builds community with a multiracial group of lesbians who socialize about a myriad of topics, including race, sexuality, and religion. The women even offer Donnetta advice about reconciling her conflict with sexuality and religion.

> WHITE DYK*: You know, Donnetta—god, fried tofu and sea salt. That's all you need really—The bible has been manipulated historically as a means to oppress women and blacks, and the Christian right hates gays, and why would you *want* to worship a white male glorified westernized depiction of God?
>
> BLACK DYK*: Yeah, you need to look to your African roots and become a true part of the same gender loving daughters of the Diaspora! I have been trying to get you to come to our drumming circle for months now. (24)

Humor aside, Donnetta is not sure about her friends' suggestions that she abandon religion, become queerer, and more Afrocentric, but she begins to think about God and religion in more expansive ways.

This newfound view of faith allows her to focus on her newly acquired girlfriend, named Girlfriend. She tells the audience, "When I closed my eyes as a kid this was the woman I imagined. Her. Complex, different, soulful. She even shares my views on spirituality and we share glorious lazy Sunday mornings in bed, in each other's arms. Look at what God has given me. This is the one" (25). With Girlfriend, Donnetta appears less conflicted and more comfortable with her faith and sexuality than she once was. There are moments of genuine love and acceptance. On Donnetta's birthday, Girlfriend presents her with a belt buckle as a gift. Donnetta then says "I love you" to a woman for the first time and, in doing so, transfers some of the devotion she had for God to her lover. That is not to say she no longer has faith in God—she does—but this is the first time she invests emotionally in a female lover. She acknowledges the constraints of religion—that to be an acceptable Christian in the tradition in which she was raised, she would have to perform femininity and heterosexuality daily. That is, she would have to speak what bell hooks calls "the right speech of womanhood," and for a masculine woman exclusively attracted to women, it would be a dishonest, soul-crushing speech. Leaving her calling behind, she puts all of her devotion into her relationship in a demonstration of resistance to the compulsory embodiment of a regional version of Black womanhood.

Girlfriend and Donnetta's story is not a fairy tale, however. (In fact, neither she nor Bulldagger "get the girl.") Over time, Donnetta becomes ambivalent toward Girlfriend and abandons her emotionally. The ambivalence stems from her (and Bulldagger's) hypermasculine tendency to worship the femme body. Donnetta describes the Girlfriend's physique before her personality because that is what attracts her first. The fault is not her appreciation for the beauty of a feminine body; it is her inability to see the woman beyond its surface. Girlfriend's body becomes a metaphorical altar to which Donnetta prays. Taking on Bulldagger's characteristics, she looks to it as a source of security for her identity. It is also interesting that Girlfriend has no proper name; she is named in relation to Donnetta, in the possessive sense (*her* girlfriend), which signifies that the relationship was, is, and will continue to be out of balance. Battling deep-rooted issues—negative self-image and low self-worth, Girlfriend's discomfort with her body, especially, mimics Donnetta's. Girlfriend, too, is coming into herself while combatting insecurities that simultaneously pull Donnetta toward her and push her away. Exhibiting a toxic savior complex, Donnetta believes she can heal her lover with a kiss or a touch, but this kind of lovin' on, she soon finds, is not a cure-all for Girlfriend's pain. During their subsequent breakup, Donnetta initiates the separation, voicing that she has grown bored of the predictability of their roller-coaster relationship. Girlfriend interrupts, takes the power in the scene, and delivers an astute reading of her own.

> GIRLFRIEND: Shut up! Oh my God you were just waiting for this. Anything.
> DONNETTA: You can go out, meet new pe—
> GIRLFRIEND: You don't get to dictate how I move through this. You don't control that, I do. (27)

Hurt, Girlfriend exposes the truth of Donnetta's contradictory behaviors in love. In one breath, Donnetta proclaims that she has found heaven in the lover (Girlfriend)—referring to her body as the cartography of heaven—and in the next breath, she ends the relationship. Until this moment, Donnetta's has been the pronounced voice in the couple's narrative. However, the femme, here, reads the butch, taking her inventory and demanding radical honesty. Reflecting on faith, fantasy, and love, Donnetta confesses: "Having faith in what is unseen actually comes a lot easier than standing in judgment of a beating heart you can feel. A mouth you can taste. It isn't being patched through to a higher power through a figmented middle-man" (27). Lovin' on a flesh-and-blood person who talks back "hits different" than lovin' an omniscient God that requires faith alone or trusting the interpretation of his interlocutors.

Donnetta is clearly teachable; she is still growing, and although she has other relationships with women after Girlfriend, her love life remains a work in progress. In denying her protagonist a happy ending, Grays maps out an alternative route home for the Black queer woman, and it is a solo trip.

The cowboy Donnetta idealizes and idolizes is not only unattainable but disruptive to her personal relationships. In leaving Girlfriend, Donnetta leaves the butch idol behind and, for the first time, Bulldagger asks critical questions about her creator—"What does one do when she has told God no thanks? When she has turned away from lovers whose collective love could fill the cosmos?" (28). Donnetta returns home—that is, she returns to her childhood home in South Carolina. While there, she engages in quotidian activities with her mother, such as washing and hanging laundry. Being near her mother's body represents safety, and Donnetta, as if seeing her for the first time, notices the strength of the female and the feminine. She says, "Her breasts tell of a history of giving. I see scars. I see moles, stretch marks and lines that aren't lines. They are movements and storytellers that invite you to sit for a long while and listen to them. I mean she is . . . true softness, caring, and a safe place to stay" (29). Her mother's figure and its markings tell stories that yearn for a listening ear. And who better than a playwright and performer in search of her authentic self to receive them?

Pariah: Legacy

Screenwriter-director Dee Rees did not begin her professional life as a filmmaker. Like Ava DuVernay, who worked in marketing and public relations at 20th Century Fox prior to becoming a filmmaker, Rees worked as a marketing assistant at Proctor & Gamble. On set during the filming of a commercial for a company product, she asked someone in production how to become a filmmaker and they told her to go to film school. And she did. Well into her twenties, she moved to New York City to attend New York University's Graduate Film program, where she was mentored by Spike Lee, who gave her feedback on scripts and later served as an executive producer of her debut film *Pariah,* a coming-out story about a Black queer girl living in New York City.

While *Pariah* is not the first film of its kind, it is a groundbreaking film that is the first to garner praise and attention on a wide scale. The film centers on Black queer girlhood and the obstacles to womanhood in an early twenty-first-century story that is unique yet relatable to the lived experience of Black queer people raised in religious households in a time in which they have the freedom to explore sexuality and gender expression in less conservative ways.

Pariah is personal for Rees because, prior to moving to New York, she came out to her parents as a lesbian. They did not take it well. Again, Southern Black families often struggle to embrace their queer kids without conditions because of the belief that homosexuality is a sin and that sin should be avoided, even if the sinner is one's child. Moving far away from the South, as Donnetta's journey shows, is not an uncommon leap for queer Southerners. Having been raised in Antioch, Tennessee (near Nashville), Rees has said that one of the first things she noticed in New York City was that queer kids were able to express themselves queerly, a far different experience than she had as an adolescent: "I got called 'dyk*y' and 'butch' in high school, and teased for the way I walked, so I went out of my way to avoid seeming gay, just tried to be girly and fit in."[17] It is from these combined experiences that Rees wrote *Pariah,* which focuses on a teenager named Alike (played by Adepero Oduye) who, like Rees, is trying to fit into two different worlds.

When *Pariah* premiered at the Sundance Film Festival in 2011, it was a critical success, garnering numerous awards including Sundance's Excellence in Cinematography Award, an NAACP Image Award, the John Cassavetes Award at the Film Independent Spirit Awards, and the Freedom of Expression Award from the National Board of Review. Attributing the success of Black lesbian filmmakers in Hollywood to the festival circuit, Yvonne Welbon says, in a roundtable discussion between women-of-color film scholars, "There are about 130 of these festivals worldwide right now. The film festival has historically been the first stop for a new filmmaker. Festival directors have a lot of power in selecting the next generation of filmmakers."[18] *Pariah*'s early success, even as a short film, reflects the potential of film festivals to launch nontraditional films to mainstream visibility. In 2021 *Pariah* made history as the first film by a Black queer woman to be included in the highly regarded Criterion Collection. In an interview with Rebecca Keegan of the *Hollywood Reporter,* Rees admits, "I maybe shouldn't be the first. Maybe it should have been Julie Dash. I would start with that acknowledgement, but it doesn't diminish the pride I feel."[19] Humbly, Rees acknowledges the omission of a pre-eminent director of Black feminist/womanist cinema and nods to Dash's influence on her own work.

Since its release in 1991, film scholars have written at length about Julie Dash's pioneering independent film, and only feature film to date, *Daughters of the Dust.* Dash's significance as one of the few Black women filmmakers of the 1990s Black Cinema era cannot be overstated, a fact of which Rees is well

17. Zack, "'Pariah' a Daring Coming of Age Story," 1.
18. Keeling et al., "*Pariah* and Black Independent Cinema," 426.
19. Keegan, "Director Dee Rees," 1.

aware.[20] Before Rees, there were other writer-directors such as Cheryl Dunye, whose 1996 documentary-style comedy *The Watermelon Woman* was the first feature film directed by an out Black lesbian.[21] Welbon, reflecting on prior films, notes, "The 1974 student Academy Award–winning short *Sojourn*, codirected by Michelle Parkerson and Jimi Lyons Jr., is thought to be the first film directed by an out Black [lesbian] filmmaker. . . . It is the 1986 video 'Women in Love, Bonding Strategies of Black Lesbians' by Sylvia Rhue that is the first out black lesbian film about black lesbians."[22] Thus, Rees's film must be contextualized as a part of a cinematic genealogical whole in which Black queer women filmmakers' visions have been and are being captured.[23]

Rees's visual composition and Bradford Young's luscious, color-conscious cinematography are essential to the film's impact on audiences. Every frame could be a photograph. The visual storytelling is as impactful as, maybe more than, at times, the dialogue in the film. Like many independent films, what is unsaid is as affecting and dynamic as what is said. The vibrant color palate of deep blues, saturated purples, and magentas is a visual delight that represents Alike's worldview. The colors become more natural and brighter at the end of the film, symbolizing her transition to adulthood. Young "shot most of the film using available light, including nighttime scenes in a bedroom using only Christmas lights and an Ikea lamp with a red lampshade."[24] Lighting the predominately Black cast well was important to him. Reflecting on the progress made in cinema regarding race and lighting, he says, "There's been a gap where not a lot of work has been done to make people of color look (on screen) like we see them in the world."[25] *Pariah* presents various shades of Black skin in their natural state. For example, Oduye's dark skin glistens in the low-lit scenes, whereas in many films, low light can make a dark-skinned person less visible. Filmmakers of color recognize that lighting matters when capturing Black people of all shades and hues (and there are many) on camera.

---

20. Black Cinema in the 1990s was robust and included "Hood" films depicting the lives and deaths of young Black men in urban geographies, such as John Singleton's *Boyz n the Hood* and the Hughes brothers' *Menace II Society.* At the same time, directors Cheryl Dunye, Dr. Ayoka Chenzira (*Alma's Rainbow*), Darnell Martin (*I Like It Like That*), Euzhan Palcy (*A Dry White Season*), Kasi Lemmons (*Eve's Bayou*), Leslie Harris (*Just Another Girl on the I.R.T.*), Maya Angelou (*Down in the Delta*), and Zeinabu Irene Davis (*Compensation*) were depicting the lives of Black and Brown women in urban and rural spaces.

21. For a thorough analysis, see Derk, "Inverting Hollywood."

22. Keeling et al., "*Pariah* and Black Independent Cinema," 425.

23. See Welbon and Juhasz, *Sisters in the Life,* for more on Black lesbian cinema.

24. Lindeman, "Contender—Cinematographer Bradford Young," 1.

25. Lindeman, "Contender—Cinematographer Bradford Young," 1.

Additionally, the visual composition of the scenes also captures Alike's confusion about how to best perform queerness from a woman's perspective. She knows she is a lesbian, but she is not quite sure *how* to perform that role or *if* she should perform at all. Should she wear fitted caps, baggy clothes, sneakers, and "pack" a dildo like her best friend Laura? Or, should she wear the dresses, skirts, and blouses that her mother encourages her to wear? The answers to these questions become clearer to Alike as the film progresses but, as Christina N. Baker observes, Alike's clothing and accessories (her "gender displays") are essential to her identity development and her romantic life.[26] Whether feminine or masculine, these displays ground her in social realities inside and outside of the home and force her to maintain an unsustainable performance of self that will either break her or her families (queer and straight) apart.

The short film version opens with a quote from Audre Lorde, whose writing resonated with Rees as she drafted the screenplay: "Wherever the bird with no feet flew, she found trees with no limbs." The bird symbolizes Alike, and the people and places she encounters, save a few, represent limbless trees upon which she cannot perch, upon whom she cannot rely to support or nurture her, because of their own lack and brokenness. The first image on screen, after the quote disappears, is that of a pole dancer positioned upside down. The dancer's arm and upper back are shown in close-up as she sensually and slowly slides down the pole while a DJ plays Khia's 2001 hit "My Neck, My Back"—a rap song as raunchy in its sexual description as Lucille Bogan's upbeat blues song "Shave 'Em Dry" (1924). Alike, Laura, and a host of clubgoers are in a women's club called the "Catnip Lounge" somewhere in Brooklyn, New York; the club has recently opened and is, like many queer clubs, a welcome respite for women to meet women. Of note, Alike is on the precipice of adulthood at seventeen years old, and this is her first exposure to an exclusively adult lesbian space. Therefore, she is both uncomfortable and titillated by the dancer in front of her.

The next shot is a medium shot on Alike from the dancer's perspective, revealing the teenager in urban masculine attire as she ogles in awe at the curves and skill of the pole dancer. Then the camera slowly turns upright to Alike's perspective. Mouth agape watching the performance, Alike quickly becomes annoyed when her best friend, Laura (played by Pernell Walker), bumps into her and interrupts her visualization. The girls have a brief inaudible exchange before Alike walks away and sits down at a table near another masculine-presenting woman. Laura, who is a dominant personality, takes

26. Baker, "Rebellious Love," 144.

responsibility and pride in teaching Alike how to dress, walk, and talk like a confident stud/AG rather than a young lesbian exploring her sexuality inside and outside of the club. Alike appears discontent in clothes that do not fit her personality. She sits in the crowded club alone in deep thought; this is the first of several instances in which the quiet, introverted teenager turns inward to escape an uncomfortable reality.

The opening scene is nearly the same in the long and short versions. Of the differences in both films, Jennifer DeClue muses:

> I first encountered *Pariah* in 2007 as a short film that won the Audience Award at OutFest, Los Angeles' LGBT film festival. Since then, *Pariah* has been produced as a feature film distributed by Focus Features. The narrative differences and casting changes made between *Pariah* the short and *Pariah* the feature are indicative of industry demands for name recognition and universal appeal in this capital-generating artistic venture.[27]

DeClue prefers the rawness of the short film version, commenting on the common phenomena of changes in the script (characters, story arc) and casting when Hollywood production companies and distributors secure deals with independent filmmakers. Filmmakers want their work to reach larger audiences, but the majority of them lose some creative control along the way, having to augment the script or recast roles with known ("name") actors to appease their financiers who, understandably, are concerned about profit and recouping their investment. If losing some degree of artistic control is a given in the industry, the short film version of *Pariah* preserves qualities of Rees's narrative that are Blacker and queerer than those in the feature film.

The casting choices in the twenty-seven-minute short are, on a superficial level, more logical, and some of the personality choices and outmoded cultural behaviors of the characters are realistic, thereby heightening the tension between characters. Alike's mother, Audrey (played by Gameela Wright), and sister, Sharonda (played by Sahra Mellesse), are performed by actresses whose skin color and facial features align with Oduye's. Her father, Arthur (played by Wendell Pierce), is an antagonist in this version who becomes furious when he learns that Alike has been exploring lesbianism and butch embodiment. Physically imposing, he gets in her face, threatening to "whip her ass" as a corrective method. Blaming Audrey, he instructs her not to call Alike by her nickname "Lee" because "that's what the fuckin' problem is now." Lee is a more masculine name and, by his homophobic logic, the mother is

27. Keeling et al., "*Pariah* and Black Independent Cinema," 424.

responsible for the daughter being queer; therefore, continuing to call her by a man's name encourages their daughter's queer behaviors. This Arthur's aggression toward Alike compared to the mild manner and easygoing parenting of the character (as played by Charles Parnell) in the feature film highlights a significant shift in the domestic dynamics. Parnell's Arthur is kind and loving toward Alike, presenting a markedly different type of Black father figure than is often made accessible on screen: one that is nurturing and protective of his child, regardless of her sexuality or gender expression. It also casts Audrey (as played by Kim Wayans in the feature film) as a kind of villain.

Mother's Milk

Both versions of *Pariah* complement one another, but the feature film provides a more comprehensive view of the power struggles that many Black queer youth have with their parents and surrogate family members as they become more independent. Repositioning the mother figure in opposition to the queer child figure is a thought-provoking choice reflected in Alike and Audrey's relationship (see figure 5), as well as that of Laura and her mother. When their mothers reject them, it reads as a painful emotional attack on two girls who, going the extra mile to meet their homophobic mothers halfway, are left empty-handed, craving their love and support—their *mother's milk*. Mothers are expected to nurture their children, but it is important to recognize that not all mothers have a maternal instinct or desire. Some mothers are more adept at parenting children of a younger age rather than teenagers. A biological mother is usually the child's first home, the first body in/on which they literally find comfort. It seems counterintuitive that a mother would throw a child away after raising them for seventeen years. Thus, the portrayal of two mothers rejecting their daughters is doubly devastating to the characters and the audience.

In Alike's home, her Bible-toting mother has taught her that a "good" Christian girl is a heterosexual girl. Audrey suspects that her daughter is queer and becomes increasingly adamant that Alike dress and act more feminine like her younger sister, Sharonda, and her co-worker's daughter, Bina—who ironically has queer tendencies and becomes Alike's first girl crush and sexual experience. In a Black, middle-class, religious, conservative family that appears to be the picture of the African American Dream, Alike's queerness would put a stain on the family name, and call into question, as Jennifer DeClue puts it, their "national belonging." Alike's "condition" has the potential to ruin a façade that the family has so carefully constructed for the benefit

FIGURE 5. Kim Wayans (*left*) and Adepero Oduye (*right*) in *Pariah,* 2011. Courtesy of NBC Universal.

of outsiders looking in. Reading Candice Jenkins's *Private Lives, Proper Relations,* DeClue says, "Jenkins argues that ideologies of upward mobility and the salvific wish that separates Alike from her parents is visualized in *Pariah* in a cinematic eruption that lays open the sorrow and the stakes of not belonging and not being willing or able to help it."[28] While Alike's sorrow is evident, a good portion of that sorrow stems from her parents' noxious untethering.

Audrey's mistreatment of Alike as she begins to break out of the cocoon of their household bothers Alike's father. He is simultaneously protective of his tomboyish daughter and disgusted by his wife. Their marriage is falling apart, and he may be having an affair, which creates more tension between the two and leads them to put Alike in the middle of their troubled marriage. It may seem as if Alike is the problem, but it is conceivable that Audrey views her as the solution to the fracture. Correcting Alike's queerness with the support of her husband may be a way to mend their broken marriage. If they can agree that Alike, and girls like her, are nasty, deviant, sinful (but "save-able"), and if they can collectively correct that wrong, then they can find common ground and save their marriage. What Audrey does not account for, however, is her husband's unconditional love for his child—a *storge* love that she is incapable of showing.

Arthur, who is shown bonding with Alike over basketball and other parent–child activities like teaching her to drive, sees nothing wrong with Alike or her behaviors. Audrey pronounces that Alike is changing—staying out late,

28. Keeling et al., "*Pariah* and Black Independent Cinema," 424.

talking back, and keeping a strap-on and boyish clothes in her closet—and ascertains that Laura is responsible for influencing Alike to "[turn] into a damn man." The anger that Audrey exhibits, it should be noted, is comparable to the aggression that Arthur displays toward her during their arguments. Tender and playful with Alike and Sharonda, contrastingly he is quite hostile toward Audrey. There are no signs of love left in their marriage and no indication that he will agree with her and admonish Alike. This leaves the wife and mother dismissed, alone, and frustrated. Observing the couple closely evinces the ways in which they use their child to lash out at one another and to express their mutual discontent in the relationship. If Alike is the problem, then one of them must be to blame. To varying degrees, they tear each other and their daughters down due to the shame associated with the eldest child's perceived boyishness and lesbianism. Unable to sway Arthur, and in order to maintain some semblance of control, Audrey leans into religion in hopes that her faith will reunify her family. Her religiosity leads her to determine that Alike's sexuality, rather than her husband's probable infidelity, is the primary cause of the marital strife. Considering the inner workings of the turmoil at home and her centrality to it, it is understandable that Alike relies on a queer friend, Laura, for support and, later, refuge.

An out stud, Laura has a peripheral yet portentous Black queer storyline.[29] Her disapproving mother has kicked her out of the house and refuses to talk to her. In the short film, Laura is still in high school, but in the feature film, she has dropped out to work full time to support herself. Adaptive forms of survival, such as leaving school for the workforce, moving in with a friend's family, or living on the street, are not unusual for queer kids in urban spaces whose families disapprove of their so-called lifestyles. It is interesting that these parents believe that releasing their children to the world with no resources or safety net is a motivating factor in their assimilating to a straight lifestyle. As I mentioned in the introduction to this book, queer youth often hold resentments toward their disapproving family members and find other families and spaces to call home—some of which are safe and others of which are unsafe. While tough love has its place with young people, love has to enter the room at some point. Laura's mother, for example, behaves as if she hates her daughter. Desperately wanting her mother's approval, Laura, who is focusing on studying for the General Education Development test, arrives at her mother's doorstep—the doorstep of a place she used to call home—to tell her about it. The mother barely speaks at all before she slams the door. The look

---

29. See Lane-Steele, "Studs and Protest-Hypermasculinity," for an intriguing ethnographic study of studs in South Carolina.

of hurt and rejection on Laura's face, beautifully played by Walker, is uncomfortable to watch because their relationship does not have to be this way. If a choice has been made, it is the choice the mother makes to keep Laura out of her life.

Knowing the weight of such rejection, Laura embraces Alike and teaches her all she knows about being a lesbian, including how to dress, act, and reproduce other rituals of studhood (such as "throwing ones" at the newly opened lesbian strip club in town and packing a dildo). The conflict between the friends, as depicted in the first scene, is rooted in the fixedness of Laura's concept of the performance of lesbian as either that of a stud or a femme. This perspective ignores Alike's developing queer aesthetic. Laura genuinely expresses her gender in a masculine way, but Alike is not comfortable mimicking her friend's embodiment; something about it doesn't feel right. Afraid or unwilling to be honest with Laura, Alike oscillates from stud to femme clothing to a dizzying effect. Underneath the clothes, she is still the sensitive, pensive, teenage girl who wants to be loved on without conditions, but as long as she lives in her family's household, she must juggle identities between home, church, school, and the club. If she does not, she, too, is at risk of becoming unhoused.

Alike's truth finally comes to the surface when she returns home to find her parents fighting about her again. This fight forces her to admit to her parents that she is a lesbian. Perceiving this utterance of confirmation as disrespectful, Audrey loses the little control she has left, and physically attacks Alike. Again, she is taking her frustration with Arthur out on her daughter. This inciting incident forces the child to leave the home and live with Laura temporarily. This act of physical violence (of an adult putting hands on a child instead of lovin' on them through an embrace that reinforces their commitment to caring for them) is the breaking point for Alike; she is no longer safe in her home of origin and must, instead, lean on community to ensure her survival. Like Sakia Gunn before her, a life-changing act of violence is committed against Alike because she dared to confirm her queer sexuality when challenged. Because the adults in her life have a lot of growing up to do, she accepts the care that Laura offers her.

During her time away from the home and the dysfunction therein, she attempts to process the rejection, and, in this new state of independence, Alike struggles, at first. As she prepares to graduate from high school, a milestone that parents or guardians usually guide their kids through, there is no adult figure to advise her on next steps and best practices. *How can she thrive without a mother's love? Without her mother's milk to nourish and sustain her as she makes one of the most important decisions of her young life?* Immersing herself in poetry, she (as the bird in Lorde's poem) finds her feet and her footing, and she plans to leave the nest that she once called home. While the limbs that were meant to hold her (her parents) were incapable, she finds new limbs to stand on. With the support of Laura and her English teacher, Mrs. Alvarado, who sees promise in her writing, she becomes strong enough to make decisions to move forward to a future of her making, in spite of what appears to be a lost, or deferred, familial relationship.

When Alike's father comes to find her on the rooftop of the building Laura works and lives in, Alike is resolute. The scene is quiet and sad, as their connection is also frayed because he did not stand up for her during the assault. He apologizes for both his and his wife's actions. She listens quietly, neither accepting nor rejecting his apology. She tells him that she has been accepted into a summer writing program at the University of California, Berkeley, and, thereafter, hopes to begin her undergraduate studies. Notably, she does not ask his permission; instead, she tells him what she will do. Alike has finally made a choice for herself. If the film ended there, it would provide a satisfying resolution to viewers—the defeated heroine gets up after being knocked down. That is a happy ending, but Rees gives us a glimpse into a Black queer reality that is also plausible and still quite common.

Meeting with her mother one last time, per her father's suggestion, before she leaves for California causes more pain than healing, but it also brings closure. Alike tells her mother "I love you," but Audrey can only say "I'll be praying for you." This gut-wrenching exchange leads Alike to write, using poetry as a balm for her hurt feelings and loss. We see her writing in her notebook, then the scene cuts to her in a classroom reading the inspired poem aloud to Mrs. Alvarado. Patricia White writes,

> The rhetoric of Alike's final speech "I am not running. I am choosing" and poem "I am broken. I am free" would be clichés were Aduye [*sic*] and Rees not so talented and sincere. The film's allegiance to "crossover" codes of character and narrative turns subcultural styles into signifiers of authenticity for art house audiences.[30]

White is correct; the language of the poem teeters on sentimentalism but never tips over into the saccharine, a choice which positions *Pariah* as a convincingly universal story. Alike is in tears as she nears the end of the poem, unapologetically taking up space and using her voice until she arrives at "I am free." She has learned that "brokenness" does not have to signal the end

30. White, "Pariah (2011)," 138.

of her story; it can be a "jumping-off point" for the rest of her life. Her anger can be used to write her way out of a toxic home environment, to write her way through heartbreak, to write her way into a new leg of her life's journey. Boarding the bus to leave for California, she voluntarily moves forward without her mother's embrace, and it is well with her soul.

the cowboy is dying and *Pariah* expose the tensions and comforts within the Black family when a queer girl member comes out and of age. The depictions of queer girls coming out is akin to watching an amateur tightropewalker perform without a safety net. Inspired by Black queer everyday folk and Black artists who paved the way for their works, many of whom did not have the same opportunities to publicize the narrative worlds of their queer dreams, Grays and Rees imagine futures that push the boundaries of identity, style, and aesthetic in ways that speak to their generation and future generations. The works also honor the butch girls, AGs, studs, and bois, like Sakia Gunn, whose lives were tragically cut short by those who deemed them unworthy of a future. In the spirit of transformation, healing, and the transference of generational knowledge, the next chapter begins where my own Black queer feminist consciousness began—with the radical Black lesbian feminist poetry of Staceyann Chin.

CHAPTER 4

Making It Solo

The Radical Crossings of Staceyann Chin

Staceyann Chin is a Jamaican Chinese American, lesbian, feminist performance artist and activist who was a featured poet on HBO's *Def Poetry Jam* and the Tony award–winning *Russell Simmons Def Poetry Jam on Broadway.*[1] She has written and performed four original solo plays—*Hands Afire* (2000), *Unspeakable Things* (2001), *Border/Clash* (2005), and *MotherStruck!* (2015)—and a multitude of poems in the slam and spoken-word traditions.[2] As a resident artist, guest speaker, and workshop facilitator, she has traveled to arts venues and educational institutions around the globe. Chin's performances are consistently passionate, humorous, and explicit, reading more like survival guides than entertainment.

Since the 1990s, Chin has made a career of exploring the most pivotal and vulnerable moments of her life. The 2024 documentary film, *A Mother Apart,* directed by Laurie Townshend, follows Chin and her then-ten-year old daughter, Zuri, over seven years, as Chin revisits the circumstances of her mother Hazel's abandonment of her and her brother Delano when she

1. *Russell Simmons's Def Poetry Jam* ran on Broadway from 2002 to 2003 at the Longacre Theater in New York City. For more on the Broadway production, see chapter 4, "*Def Poetry Jam,*" in Dolan, *Utopia in Performance.*

2. Chin won numerous slams in her early career, including the 1998 Lambda Literary Foundation's National Poetry Slam and the 1999 Women of Color Conference's National Poetry Slam.

was ten years old. *MotherStruck!* depicts her attempts to conceive a child as a single lesbian without adequate health insurance. Her 2009 memoir, *The Other Side of Paradise,* described by Jocelyn Fenton Stitt as "the first book-length piece of life writing to chronicle growing up lesbian in Jamaica," details both heartbreaking and hilarious stories from Chin's childhood to early adulthood, including her forced migration to New York City after she was sexually assaulted for being an out lesbian.[3] Stitt writes, "Staceyann's lesbian identity as a young adult provokes hostility and violence that cannot be separated from the neglect and trauma she experiences as a child because of her outspokenness, her racial identity, and her female body."[4] In "Disciplining the Unruly (National) Body in Staceyann Chin's *The Other Side of Paradise,*" Stitt rightly connects Chin's experiences of abuse not simply to the hyper-religiosity of the Caribbean but also to a history of colonization and enslavement that has impacted generations of Black Jamaican families.

For decades, Chin has documented her life through poetry with brutal honesty and authenticity. These complex time capsules of masterfully written first-person accounts and reflections on citizenship, aging, lesbianism, womanness, war, hate, grief, loneliness, erotic escapades, art, and Black feminist thought are most poignantly embodied by the artist herself. In 2009 I attended a reading and book signing event for *The Other Side of Paradise* at Outwrite Bookstore in Atlanta, Georgia, because I wanted to witness firsthand how the petite woman with the big voice and unshakable spirit could move a room. A captivating performer, even when she is reading excerpts from her book, her voice, polemical perspectives, and "mother tongue" seep into your bones and remain there long after she is gone. Audiences are not required to agree with Chin's literary descriptions of the infinite ways she loves on herself and other bodies, which range from erotic to spiritual to political to platonic to familial expressions, to be impressed by her vision of a free and fair society. One is not required to agree with her delivery, which is often, but not always, markedly direct. One is not required to do much of anything except bear witness; however, audiences are often roused by the speaker and the speech, moved to identify the social problems for which they want change.

In this chapter, I study the radical Black lesbian-feminist writings of Staceyann Chin in an effort to chart a trajectory of lifetime acts of lovin' on by claiming space for herself and other minoritarian subjects using sites of protest that include the theater, the urban city, and the rural countryside. In my analyses of Chin's poetry, plays, prose, and motherwork, I attend to how one

3. Stitt, "Disciplining the Unruly (National) Body," 2.
4. Stitt, "Disciplining the Unruly (National) Body," 1.

Afro-Asian Caribbean American lesbian-feminist performance artist creates home(s) in the face of bewildering contradictions, mixed cultural messages, and other obstacles to comfort in the US and the Caribbean.

Intersections

In a 2011 talk at City University of New York, Staceyann Chin, moving in and out of patois, describes her understanding of intersectionality to an audience of undergraduate students as follows: "Intersectionality just means that you have more than one thing dat concern you. Like, you're black and you're lesbian and you're poor. And you're—y'know, like the more shit you have wrong with you, the more intersectionality *is* you."[5] She alludes to an intersectional life experience that brings her race, gender, class, nationality, and sexuality together to shape an identity that is an amalgamation of sorts. Performance poetry allows her to unpack the intersections of her identity and explore the depth of feeling attached to it. As a Black queer woman, it also allows her to flex her authorial voice, synthesize culture and unpack specific experiences of oppression on paper, and manifest her worldview in public space. Through solo performance forms like slam poetry, spoken word, and plays, she animates instances in which her personhood is respected and moments when it is disregarded as culturally inauthentic or wholly insignificant.

Crucially, she observes—as persons seeking liberation do—that authoritative bodies (such as family members, friends, teachers, and employers) have imposed expectations of respectable performances of identity upon her. Her definition of intersectionality speaks to a Black queer feminist standpoint that maintains that identification is a process of defining oneself for oneself. With an irony unique to her direct personality, bold assertions, and physical performance style, Chin identifies her race (Black), sexuality (lesbian), and class upbringing (poor, or working class) as "problems" that hold significant meaning in society. These so-called problems (Blackness, queerness, and financial insecurity) are not *her* "problems"; they are society's "problems" *with her.* Understanding intersectionality—what it is and what it is not—is of utmost importance when considering the needs of those of us (the majority of people) who are not the "mythical norm."[6]

---

5. Chin, "2nd Annual Student Research Day."

6. Lorde, "Age, Race, Class, and Sex," 108. According to Lorde, the "mythical norm" is "usually defined as white, thin, male, young, heterosexual, Christian, and financially secure" (108).

Kimberlé Williams Crenshaw's theory of *intersectionality* has been challenged in constructive ways by feminist scholars like Jennifer C. Nash to expand its meanings and applications, but critical race theory is now under attack by conservative lawmakers seeking to pass legislation delegitimizing the study of race and deinstitutionalizing Black history from school curricula.[7] In "the intersectionality wars," Jane Coasten of *Vox* writes, "there may not be a word in American conservatism more hated right now than 'intersectionality.'"[8] Coasten investigates the rise of anti-CRT rhetoric, sitting down with Crenshaw to discuss the origins of intersectionality, its mainstream appeal, and the conservative backlash to it. In 2021 Texas Governor Greg Abbott signed a bill into law banning critical race theory from being taught in primary and secondary public schools in the state. Similarly, in 2022 Governor Ron DeSantis signed the "Don't Say Gay" bill into law in Florida banning the discussion of sexual orientation and gender identity in public primary schools. Shunning "woke" culture, conservative lawmakers argue that critical race theory should not even be taught in state colleges and universities—as if discussions of inequality, privilege, and society's responsibility to practice a level of consideration of others (regardless of race, class, gender, sexuality, etc.) can be scrubbed from the zeitgeist with the stroke of a pen. Coasten explains, "To Crenshaw, the most common critiques of intersectionality . . . are actually affirmations of the theory's fundamental truth: that individuals have individual identities that intersect in ways that impact how they are viewed, understood, and treated."[9]

The complexities of identity and perception are concerns for transnational Black lesbians like Staceyann Chin. They are considerations for all subjects who cannot or choose not to identify as one identity or another and who, like Chin, resist the very notion of authenticity by emphasizing the complexities of a variegated existence. E. Patrick Johnson finds that the benefit of identity "performed and experienced as real" is that "it constitutes a legitimate way through which subjects maintain control over their lives and their image."[10] Chin's work demonstrates a constant reformatting of self that is intentional but also natural to her approach to an activist and nomadic life. She has no desire to assimilate to normative notions of any kind—be it notions of what it means to be Black, lesbian, mother, artist, woman, Jamaican, American, poet, or writer. To be understood, Chin's unruly performances require an intersectional lens to deconstruct, analyze, and reassemble her many selves.

7. See Nash, *Black Feminism Reimagined.*

8. Coasten, "Intersectionality Wars," 1.

9. Coasten, "Intersectionality Wars," 1.

10. E. Johnson, *Appropriating Blackness,* 18.

"Cross-Fire"

Chin's performance poems exemplify the precarious nature of home for Afro-Caribbean lesbians coming out, coming of-age, and making space for themselves in regions of the Americas whose societies challenge, reject, and embrace their identifications in contradictory ways. In a recorded performance of "Cross-Fire" circa 2010, Chin stands in front of a microphone wearing army green cargo pants, an orange spaghetti-strap tank top, and a few pieces of jewelry.[11] She wears no makeup and rocks a parted Afro hairdo. At 5 feet tall and 110 pounds, she holds nothing back. With grand physical movements and gestures, Chin forces energy out through all of her limbs. A consummate professional, when she makes an error in the text, she does not draw attention to it, she simply pushes through with flat palms parallel to the stage floor. She forces the carefully crafted words, phrases, and sentences out of her mouth using all of her articulators (lips, teeth, tongue) to become one with the text. The more intense her words of protest, the more her arms flail deliberately emphasizing with passionate intention each social issue she is for or against.

"Cross-Fire"—a thought experiment on cultural identity politics—is one of many poems that exemplify Chin's dexterity with writing about identity in intersectional terms in only a few pages. In performance, she uses her small body and fast-paced, Jamaican-accented vocal delivery to grab hold of spectators and refuses to let them go until she has had the last word. The poem begins with a student questioning the poet's sexual and feminist identifications. Interpreting the student, she projects: "Am I a feminist / or a womanist / the student needs to know / if I do men occasionally / and primarily am I a lesbian."[12] The student, here, is representative of a culture that compulsorily and uncritically relies on binaries to maintain order. The question raised by "the student," as Chin reads it, pertains primarily to Chin's sexuality. The student "needs to know" the label she prefers in order to identify (read categorize) the poet as lesbian or heterosexual. If the student can compartmentalize Chin, then the poet may be more comprehensible to her (less radical, less intimidating).

Understanding the similarities and differences of feminism and womanism, Chin has difficulty being forthright with the student. Although she calls herself a Black feminist, womanism is also a part of her practice. Her intersectional approach to thinking, writing, and speaking about political

11. Chin, "Staceyann Chin: Feminist or Womanist."

12. Chin, "Staceyann Chin: Poet for the People," 366.

and personal issues aligns with feminism and womanism, in keeping with Alice Walker's original definition that "womanist is to feminist as purple is to lavender."[13] She is equally as concerned about the livelihoods of queer people as she is people living with HIV/AIDS in the United States and abroad; with violence against and between Black youth in urban spaces; with women's reproductive rights; and with people's ability to access affordable healthcare.[14] All things considered, there are a host of issues that she cares about, and her Black queer feminist and womanist ethics inform her arts-activism.

Chin's intersectional epistemology is important to her, and she is dogmatic about performing that knowledge in nonhierarchical terms, an approach that requires audiences to pay close attention to the many thematic shifts throughout her poetry. These shifts are intentional. They are strategic. They are meant to disturb the spectator, to shake up their perceptions of race, gender, sexuality, religion, nation and other identificatory categories. Thus, when she responds to the student by turning lesbianism—which is the topic she perceives is at the heart of the student's question—on its head, she does so by illustrating the extent to which identity can be messy, especially when Blackness, queerness, and womanness intersect.

> This business of dyk*s and dyk*ry I tell her
> is often messy
> with social tensions as they are
> you never quite know what you're getting
> —girls who are only straight at night
> —hardcore butches who sport dresses
> between nine and six during the day
> sometimes she is an endangered chameleon
> trapped by the limitations of our imagination[15]

It is obvious that Chin is dodging the question because she does not trust the student to see her beyond "the limitations of [their] imagination." By not divulging outright that she is a lesbian, Chin is exercising caution and protecting herself from potential backlash. In another poem, "Poet for the People," she admits that, like the women she describes in the excerpt above, she is sometimes fearful of identifying as a lesbian, even in so-called safe spaces. As a result of this justified fear, she engages in a practice of self-care by being deliberate about how and with whom she chooses to self-identify. Therefore,

13. Walker, *In Search of Our Mother's Gardens,* xii.
14. Chin, "Staceyann Chin: Poet for the People," 366.
15. Chin, "Staceyann Chin: Poet for the People," 366.

Chin replies to the student by voicing concern about sexual assault against women, a problem that concerns Chin and should, arguably, concern the young female student:

> primarily I tell her
> I am concerned about young women
> who are raped on college campuses
>   in cars
> after poetry readings like this one
>   in bars[16]

People tend to gravitate toward sensational topics such as sexuality as opposed to immediate life concerns like sexual assault; therefore, Chin strategically redirects the conversation from the student's personal "need to know" to political issues that affect the larger society. Chin continues describing the continued victimization that many abused women experience, noting how their stories are often distrusted and their experiences questioned when or if they report sexual and physical assault. Her firsthand experience with sexual intimidation and assault informs the intensity of her advocacy for abuse survivors.

As quickly as Chin clarifies to the female student that she cares about women and their right to simply be in the world without fear of victimization, she turns to a male student to discuss the topic of religion. In her exchange with him, which is more monologue than dialogue, she is able to illustrate the power of people's "cultural assumptions" about identity. Chin speaks the words of "the boy in the double-X hooded sweatshirt"[17] as he gives an explicitly subversive reading of Jesus's identity:

> that blond haired blue eyed Jesus in the Vatican ain't right
> that motherfucker was Jewish, not white
> Christ was a Middle Eastern Rastaman
> who ate grapes in the company of prostitutes
> and drank wine more than he drank water[18]

Transitioning to her own voice, Chin writes:

> born of the spirit the disciples also loved him in the flesh
> but the discourse is on people who clearly identify as gay

16. Chin, "Staceyann Chin: Poet for the People," 366.
17. Chin, "Staceyann Chin: Poet for the People," 367.
18. Chin, "Staceyann Chin: Poet for the People," 367–68.

or lesbian or straight
the State needs us to be a clear left or right
those in the middle get caught in the cross-fire away at the other side[19]

As a writer, Chin holds the attention of the students by inserting controversial critiques of religious history. As a performer, she embodies the students. She recites this passage in the boy's voice, which softens her slam of religiosity and government. Religion becomes an intermediary—a placeholder—to maintain her audience's focus while she simultaneously discusses two or more issues she is invested in changing.

Commenting on partisanship, Chin critiques the tendency of people to make assumptions without considering the precarity of history and knowledge. If there are limits to what we can know about the past, then we should question what we think we know, as opposed to blindly accepting those assumptions as Truth. To be clear, the boy's interpretation of the actions and intentions of Jesus and his disciples is speculative; however, by considering the traditional interpretation of the story of Jesus alongside the boy's revisionist interpretation, the story forces audiences to question established norms and teachings. This excerpt illustrates that faith—one's belief in the unseen—can be an unstable concept. There is no straight answer to the student's primary question, and this question sparks a series of other questions that may or may not have concrete answers. This complex engagement with disparate thoughts reflects Chin's constant state of flux, in terms of identity and faith. "God," for Chin, "is that place between belief and what you name it," and that liminal space between faith and religion is where she is most comfortable as an artist, activist, and human. She writes:

never one thing or the other—
I am everything I fear
tears and sorrows
black windows and muffled screams
in the morning I am all I ever wanted to be[20]

Chin paints a picture with words of the emotional complexities of identity. Recognizing that she is always changing and that not even her chosen identifiers are stable, she embraces her future selves, and the associated processes and transformations, with fear and excitement.

19. Chin, "Staceyann Chin: Poet for the People," 368.
20. Chin, "Staceyann Chin: Poet for the People," 368.

Of identity, E. Patrick Johnson writes, "when we 'fix' and confine our identity as monolithic, we inhibit our road both to recovery from the diseases that plague our communities and to discovering our humanity."[21] If these diseases are, say, colorism, homophobia, and classism, then the remedy may be intersectional identification. Chin resists the pressure to assume a single identity, as that would not accurately capture who she is and how she moves through life at a mishmash of intersections that almost inevitably leaves her searching for a loving home where she does not have to compromise her biracial and transnational identity, queer socialist politics, feminist ethics, or free-flowing artistic impulses. Chin is constantly negotiating identity in her poetry as if it were a prerequisite for her to exist more completely in an unstable world. This effort seems exhausting, but it has become a habitual practice for her, as is evident by the unedited stream of consciousness social media posts which allow Chin to work through social issues on a digital stage, issues that only change in presentation as the years pass.

Early in her career, she used poetry to address assumptions about her race and religious affiliation. She writes, "Most people are surprised my father is Chinese—like there's some kind of preconditioned look for the half-Chinese lesbian poet who used to be Catholic but now believes in dreams."[22] Being raised Black in the Caribbean as a mixed-race person is meaningful socially and personally. In her memoir, Chin describes the privileges of colorism in Jamaica and its impact on her sense of belonging as a school-age child who was considered white because of her light skin. She realizes that there were times in her childhood, especially, when she received unearned privileges directly related to others' reverence for her skin and the meanings of value and virtue attached to it. The advantages of being mixed and the disadvantages of parental abandonment correlate in Chin's case, but her unapologetic approach to life through radical feminist art gives her the opportunity to craft a life in which she is the conscious, self-reflexive parent she never had. In the documentary film, *A Mother Apart,* Chin's daughter, Zuri, asks her, "Who was waiting for *you* to be born?" Quickly, Chin responds, "No one was waiting for me to be born."[23] There is certainty in her response but no self-pity or shame. Reclaiming her earliest trauma, she repurposes her truth to fortify herself as she fights for those who cannot fight by speaking the truths they cannot speak.[24]

---

21. E. Johnson, *Appropriating Blackness*, 18.

22. Chin, "Staceyann Chin: Poet for the People," 367.

23. See Townshend, *Mother Apart.*

24. Chin was born prematurely on the dirt floor of her grandmother's home on Christmas Day in 1972. Since birth, Chin has beaten the odds of survival; she is a fighter by nature.

In her work and life, Chin displays a keen eye and ear for analyzing and reinterpreting multiple aspects of a situation through an arts-activist framework that seriously considers epistemologies of metaphorical and literal border crossings. M. Jacqui Alexander, in *Pedagogies of Crossing*, signifying on the Middle Passage, writes, "The Crossing is also meant to evoke/invoke the crossroads, the space of convergence and endless possibility; the place where we put down and discard the unnecessary in order to pick up that which is necessary. It is that imaginary from which we dream the craft of a new compass."[25] Considering Alexander's philosophical musing on passages and passing through, as it might pertain to Chin's writing and performance work, allows me to contextualize Chin's experiences of "crossing" as maneuvering through factious ideas, conditions, and circumstances that most avoid thinking about, let alone discussing in public spaces, but which she must speak, and sometimes shout, out loud. The brilliance of Chin's cramming of interwoven issues into structured moments of thought that is meant to be performed full out (no marking) is compounded by proposed solutions. This approach to activism and movement-building, which served her well as a young artist experimenting in the New York City slam community and Broadway commercial stage, is not self-indulgent. It is a sacrifice from a place of deep commitment to applying a lovin' on ethic that is invested in the liberation of all people, especially marginalized people.

Chin puts her body at the forefront of personal narratives through which she articulates a particular Black lesbian-feminist identity and documents her process of becoming visible, autonomous, and woman-centered. If Black lesbians in most cultures are considered outliers who threaten to disrupt hegemonic patriarchy, then the act of performing Black lesbian womanhood in public space is inherently political. By positioning her body and autobiographical narratives front and center, and without spectacle, Chin claims space, if only for a short time. In performance, her becoming is personal and solitary, and audiences are welcome to watch, listen, and learn from the many lessons of her roller-coaster life; however, her healing is all her own. In other words, on stage she does not ask for permission to speak, she takes it. When she tells stories in the theater and on the slam stage, she has only her feelings, memories, and dreams to give, and she accepts the risk that, because she is a multiply marginalized person, audiences may not comprehend or listen to her points of view. To this point, in *Talking Back*, bell hooks contends that Black women have not been silenced by patriarchy; that is, when hooks was a child, she recalls the women in her orbit speaking loudly and assertively in the

25. Alexander, *Pedagogies of Crossing*, 8.

domestic space (kitchen tables, dens, living rooms). She writes, "Their voices can be heard. Certainly for Black women our struggle has not been to emerge from silence into speech but to change the nature and direction of our speech. To make a speech that compels listeners, one that is heard."[26]

Closets and Religiosity in the Caribbean

As I have shown in previous chapters, "the closet" is featured prominently in Black queer feminist performance, and while it can be limiting, it can also provide a safe space for Black lesbians to perform identity without the glare of an antiqueer gaze. It can also protect them from policies and regulations that might disenfranchise them because of their sexualities. Eve Kosofsky Sedgwick writes,

> The gay closet is not a feature only of the lives of gay people. But for many gay people it is still the fundamental feature of social life; and there can be few gay people, however courageous and forthright by habit, however fortunate in the support of their immediate communities, in whose lives the closet is still not a shaping presence.[27]

While times have changed and there is more room for people to break out of various closets that obscure their identities, the fact remains that in the African diaspora, Black queer people still struggle for acceptance, leaving many to stifle their pride to simply exist. In Black lesbian feminist performance poetry, however, Black queer feminist performance artists tend to come out on pages and stages of their choosing. They break the closet door down and slam the very idea that they must disappear into the wings of society.

Lynette Goddard writes: "Coming out is a way to counter assumptions of compulsory heterosexuality and state lesbian difference from the heterosexual norm. Not surprisingly then, coming out stories have formed a significant section of lesbian literary outputs and oral histories."[28] The process of coming out—making a public announcement (to, say, family, friends, constituents) as same-gender-loving—can be, at once, risky and rewarding. One can also be dragged out of a closet unwillingly. In September 2020, Florida gubernatorial hopeful Andrew Gillum, in an interview with journalist Tamron Hall,

26. hooks, *Talking Back*, 124.
27. Sedgwick, *Epistemology of the Closet*, 68.
28. Goddard, *Staging Black Feminism*, 114.

revealed that he was bisexual—an announcement that was a claim of identity but which, for him, seemed to be one he had accepted and articulated only after pictures of him in a hotel room lying unconscious and naked on a bathroom floor were made public; he was in the room with two men, one of whom took the photos. Despite the shock and sensationalism surrounding an elected official in what was conceivably his worst moment, Gillum's embrace of a Black bisexual identity illustrates that there are costs and benefits of coming out of the closet under duress in the South.

Coming out in any part of the world can be a difficult choice to make (that is, if one is not outed) because blatant homophobia and the threat of violence and death are legitimate concerns for citizens who think and act queerly. In the Caribbean, coming out has long been complicated due to antigay legislation that deems the practice of sex between two people of the same gender tantamount to criminality—making disclosure far more dangerous than in the US. Derek Chadee and others write:

> Another Caribbean island well-known for violent and discriminatory acts against homosexuals is Jamaica. Williams (2000, 106) noted that "Jamaica is perceived to be the most homophobic Caribbean territory. It is also a badly kept secret that Jamaica has a perceptibly vibrant gay population." . . . Conservative Christian religious beliefs prevalent in Caribbean society have been cited as the primary reason for the prohibitive legal codes in the region.[29]

While queer citizens living in the Caribbean may have support systems, historically they have not been able to be openly queer safely, as is evident by Chin's migration.[30] Still, the "vibrant gay population" of artists and activists suggests that, despite general antigay sentiment built into the law, queer citizens can and do call Jamaica home.

There has been a global move toward LGBTQ equality (with the passing of antidiscrimination and marriage equality legislation), but there is progress to be made in the Caribbean to ensure queer livability. For example, there are still active sodomy (or "buggary") laws in many countries in the region. The risks of identifying as LGBTQ or appearing queerly in public can lead to physical, emotional, and psychological injury. In *The Abominable Crime* (2013)—a documentary film about lesbians and gays in Jamaica and the homophobia

29. Chadee et al., "Religiosity, and Attitudes Towards Homosexuals," 4–5.

30. This study "revealed that people with an intrinsic religious orientation displayed more negative attitudes towards homosexuality than those with an extrinsic religious orientation" (Chadee et al., "Religiosity, and Attitudes Towards Homosexuals," 16).

they encounter—activist Maurice Tomlinson describes having to leave the country after being publicly "outed" on the front page of a Montego Bay newspaper. Like Andrew Gillum, Tomlinson was forced out of the closet when a photograph of him marrying his husband in Canada was featured in an attempt to embarrass him and bring his gay rights activism in Jamaica to an end. This kind of public outing is meant to shame and silence queer people into assimilating to heteronormativity or force them back into the closet.

Religiosity (or strong religious faith), Chadee and others find, plays a significant role in the national feeling about queer people in the Caribbean. They determine that religiosity and homophobia are enmeshed in the culture, the result of which is "an exclusive in-group" mentality that relegates homosexuals (and other queer folk) to outsider status.[31] Furthermore, they find, the idea that homosexuality is against biblical law and will cause the demise of the human race is supported by many Caribbean officials. Homophobia is also a feature of some popular entertainment. With no legal protections against physical violence and hate speech, many young queer citizens, in particular, leave the Caribbean. After being sexually assaulted by twelve boys for being an out lesbian and feminist, Staceyann Chin, then a college student, left Montego Bay for the United States. Her subsequent poetry and prose reference her experiences living as a gender and sexual minority in Jamaica, and a racial, gender, and sexual minority in the United States.

Despite being rejected by family and community in Jamaica, Chin did not settle into a position of victimhood, railing against dominant cultures whose oppressive systems she believes cannot be dismantled. Nor did she internalize this rejection. Instead, she established surrogate family units in her Brooklyn community to dismantle those systems through generative love acts. Relying on the stage as a space of refuge and performance poetry to communicate her transnational, multiracial, queer-feminist ways of knowing, she has performed autobiographical moments of ecstasy and hope ("If Only out of Vanity," "Litany of Desire"); trauma and sadness ("Haiku for My Mother," "Letter to My Father"); and frustration and anger ("On Prop 8 and Being in Jamaica," "Poem for the Gay Games") with an honesty that is unique to her, the result of which is poetry that has impacted not only Black lesbians but other queer people searching for home in the world. Local slam poetry and spoken-word venues have been safe spaces for marginalized people to "act out" identity; for Chin, who found herself in the middle of the New York City slam explosion in the early 2000s, it propelled her career as a writer.

31. Chadee et al., "Religiosity, and Attitudes Towards Homosexuals," 16.

The Slam and the Spoken Word

The poetry slam can be a home away from home for people from all walks of life. It can also help people find a community of others who craft poetry as their mode of investigating love, politics, sexuality, race, religion, nationality, citizenship, gender, and more. Combining the literary and performing arts, it relies on text, the body, time, and space to convey meaning. The poetry slam is a subcultural space, an art form, a style, and a sport that provides a place for poets to articulate identity, politics, and culture. As with any public performance, there are risks associated with performing one's original work live. A poet might be ignored, misunderstood, or dismissed as inauthentic by the crowd. Despite the risks, many poets are called to express themselves by slamming. Scholar and poet Javon Johnson writes,

> Spoken word poetry existed long before the poetry slam; the competition was a trick or a tool to draw people back into poetry. These poets belong to the lineage of radical theater, which refuses the confines of the traditional stage. They create poetic spaces everywhere: coffee shops, record stores, theaters, bars, bookstores, restaurants, homes, and community centers.[32]

Marc Smith is credited as its creator, having hosted the first slam at the Green Mill Tavern in Chicago in 1987. Smith, a white American, sought to create an accessible art form that combined music, poetry, and performance. His effort was a response to what he considered the restrictive environment of poetry in academia that left him, as a nontraditional poet, on the margins of the field. The slam has been lauded as a diverse performance venue for nontraditional voices. By celebrating the voices of people of color, queer people, women, and other minorities, the slam counters heterosexual, white, Western, elite notions about poetry. Smith has described his concept for the poetry slam as "the remarriage of the art of writing poetry with the art of performing it. Putting the two back together where they belong."[33] Although Smith is credited as having invented the poetry slam, communities of slam performers have infused the competition with Africanist cultural traditions and performance aesthetics. Scott Woods writes, "[Smith] decided to craft a show that demanded audience interaction."[34] Woods explains that Smith's intention was to provide "the audience a voice, letting the audience say if they

---

32. J. Johnson, *Killing Poetry,* 1.
33. Smith, "Slam Poetry Movement," 1.
34. Woods, "Poetry Slams," 18.

liked a poem."[35] This element of audience participation mirrors the "call-and-response" of African diasporic storytelling, religious, and ritual practices.

Michèle Foster defines call-and-response as "a type of interaction between speaker and listener(s) in which the statements (calls) are emphasized by expressions (responses) from the listener(s), in which responses can be solicited or spontaneous, and in which either the calls or responses can be expressed linguistically, musically, verbally, nonverbally, or through dance."[36] Historically, call-and-response has been used to uplift and organize marginalized people. As a tool of resistance in the fields (hollers), in the church (hymns), and on the chain gang (work songs), the emancipatory nature of call-and-response can be found in slam poetry that asks audiences to engage with the performance by responding verbally or nonverbally to moments they are organically moved by. On *Def Poetry Jam,* poets and spoken-word artists like Chin, Sarah Jones, Beau Sia, and Daniel Beaty receive immediate feedback from the audience *during* the performance rather than afterward, as they might in a traditional theater setting, giving the witnesses an opportunity to participate in a supportive manner in contrast to a talent show like "Showtime at the Apollo," where the audience might erupt in resounding applause or boos based on its perception of how "good" or "bad" the performance is.

While Smith is considered the mastermind of the slam, African American poets who have popularized it share the labor by carving out the function, style, and rhythm of modern-day slam poetry. As with most popular art forms, like jazz music and tap dance, the origins of the slam are "vexed," as Javon Johnson calls it, with some nodding to Smith as its creator and others nodding to urban youth of color in the late 1970s and '80s who rapped and rhymed on the streets of New York City. Michael Eric Dyson and R. Scott Heath trace modern-day hip-hop back to Brooklyn when it was called rap—a performance practice and pastime, and a nonviolent way for rivaling factions to settle grievances.[37] Primarily young Black and Brown males "battled" not with fists but with words, and the rapper that out-rhymed his competitor was declared the "Head Emcee" and held this moniker in the neighborhood until the next battle.[38] Unlike slam competitions, Head Emcee is not determined by scores but by communal agreement as to which rapper made the most of polyrhythms, irony, humor, allusions, texture, and call-and-response. The slam and spoken word of the late twentieth century to today is more like a

35. Woods, "Poetry Slams," 18.

36. Foster, "Using Call-and-Response," 1.

37. See Dyson, *Know What I Mean?*; and Heath, "Hip_Hop Now."

38. The term "Head Emcee" is used in Kamilah Forbes's hip-hop play, *Rhyme Deferred.* For more on hip-hop theater, see Banks, *Say Word!*

rap battle than the 1940s and '50s Beatnik poetry of Smith's time. As is evident by the popularity of *Def Poetry Jam,* the rap/hip-hop and slam communities intertwined, resulting in a brand of spoken-word akin to that of Smith's poetry slam but unique to Black and Latine cultural perspectives.

Cristin O'Keefe Aptowicz historicizes the New York City slam movement in waves, in *Words in Your Face* (2008).[39] In this book, she identifies the first-wave as 1990–96, the second wave as 1996–2001, and the third wave as 2001–7. During the second and third waves, Staceyann Chin began performing. After arriving in New York City in 1997, she quickly became a part of the local poetry scene, performing at such venues as Café LaMama and Nuyorican Poets Café. In New York Chin was able to articulate the complexities that arise when one is displaced from their country of origin, using her writing to work through those intricacies in front of receptive audiences. It makes sense that she quickly became a slam favorite early on, as her full-bodied, full-voiced performance style has theatrical dynamics. Chin found that the slam allowed her to use her gift of writing and performance ability to "[feel] powerful, and heard, and seen" in a time and place that made space for her difference.[40]

In *The Cultural Politics of Slam Poetry—Race, Identity, and Performance of Popular Verse in America* (2009), Susan B. A. Somers-Willett is interested, in part, in "how and why marginalized voices—and in particular African American voices—are received as more authentic or real than other voices at poetry slams."[41] While the cultural phenomenon of slam's popularity and predominance by poets of color is interesting, it can be traced to the origins of hip-hop. The impact of commercialism and capitalism on the authenticity of the slam is a more interesting point of study. In fact, at the end of her slam career, Chin began to question and resist the notion of "selling out."

Selling Out

The commercialization of any cultural product in a capitalist economy requires profitability, that consumers buy (into) it, which can result in the dilution of the product and potentially its artistic intent. Another result is the appropriation of the cultural product by those who fetishize it and its creators. I am thinking of hip-hop and how the Black body and the white dollar intersect in ways they did not in the musical genre's first few decades, when

39. See Aptowicz, *Words in Your Face.* For more on the Los Angeles poetry slam, see J. Johnson, "Manning Up."

40. Chin, "Staceyann Chin: Poet for the People," 362.

41. Somers-Willett, *Cultural Politics of Slam,* 8.

the music circulated in Black and Brown communities in the North.[42] While commercial attention can draw more audiences to performance poetry and spotlight minorities who use the form to communicate their concerns, the cost can be the raw quality of the performance and the liberatory intent of the message. Judith Butler claims: "Just as metaphors lose their metaphoricity as they congeal through time into concepts, so subversive performances always run the risk of becoming deadening clichés through their repetition and, most importantly, through their repetition within commodity culture where 'subversion' carries market value."[43]

The paradox is that commercialism can offer slam and spoken-word artists financial stability. However, the need for financial security and (at times) public recognition may force an artist to compromise their value systems and creativity. Chin's radical artistry is an intervention into the absence of Black queer presence in mainstream performance poetry, especially in the late 1990s and early 2000s, but "going commercial" (playing for/into the white gaze and aesthetic) would limit the content and delivery of her writing. Rightly, Soyica Diggs Colbert observes that "the economics of theatrical production has yet to produce a financially viable model that also supports formal intervention and experimentation" to the conundrum Black artists find themselves in when they want to advance their careers in theater but must conform to a white gaze and aesthetic to make a living.[44]

The commercialism of the slam, in part, led Chin to transition away from the competition circuit. In her writing about choosing to leave the slam, she does not express regret about performing in the Broadway adaptation of the *Def Poetry Jam* HBO show, but she rightly observes that commercialized performance tends to transform the "people's poetry" into what Peggy Phelan calls "something other than performance."[45] Phelan's view of performance as ontological is useful here. She defines performance as having a "life [that is only] in the present": "Performance cannot be saved, recorded, documented, or otherwise participate in the circulation of representations of representations: once it does so, it becomes *something other than performance.* To the degree that performance attempts to enter the economy of reproduction it betrays and lessens the promise of its own ontology."[46] Here, Phelan posits that performance suffers as a product of the commercial machine and loses

42. See Clift, *Blacking Up,* for a documentary that explores the history of white appropriation of Black art. See also Rose, *Hip Hop Wars.*

43. Butler, *Gender Trouble,* xxi.

44. Carpenter et al., "Black Theater, Under Pressure," 24.

45. Phelan, *Unmarked,* 146.

46. Phelan, *Unmarked,* 146. Emphasis mine.

its "realness"—its freshness, its immediacy to attract, inform, and affect spectators. In my view, this is a serious problem for cultural art forms created in marginalized communities in the digital age when the notion of ownership and intellectual property are flimsy.

When spoken word is extracted from its original communal context, an element of redundancy sets in, resulting in a formula that does nothing more than please audiences. Poets uninterested in formulaic art might believe that their creativity, as a product of their identity, runs the risk of being compromised for the sake of mainstream theatrical aesthetics. For a Broadway audience, the premise and presentation of the local poetry slam is reformulated into a spectacle of itself that audiences pay large sums of money to see. In fact, these audiences expect the same entertainment night after night (and year after year). Chin writes:

> To be fair, poetry hit its stride before Russell Simmons wrapped his name and his money around it, but the media hadn't gotten a hold of it yet. . . . Then came the cameras, and unseasoned poems were quickly seasoned or laid to rest. Funny ones were fished out, and "the revolution" was made more palatable with comedy and recognizable diversity.[47]

The revolutionary rhetoric in slam poetry, she points out, has been appropriated for capitalistic gain. For Chin, the "talk" of revolution (as opposed to the action) desensitizes audiences to the very "real" social issues put forth by slam poets. In other words, spectators do not leave the commercial "slam theatre" mobilized to act in response to the social issues presented as problems in the performance; they simply leave . . . satisfied and unmoved to act. Somers-Willett notes Chin's subversive poem "I Don't Want to Slam" as a signal of her impending exit from the genre. Chin was a member of the louderArts slam team during both the 1999 and 2000 New York National Poetry Slams (NPS). In "I Don't Want to Slam," a poem written for the final round of the 2000 NPS, Chin struggles through concepts of identity and authenticity in the increasingly commercial poetry slam that are, to her, diluting the explicit content, direct message, and immediacy of spoken word. Somers-Willett reads the poem as a cry of resistance to the industrialization of the art form and the formulaic patterns that Chin finds herself and others falling into in the sport. Chin wants to write,

> poems that don't care

47. Chin, "Almost Famous," 22.

about the meter or the rhyme
poems that really couldn't give
a flying fuck about the time.[48]

Wanting more for her art, the rebel poet critiques the institution which, inarguably, made her famous. It is clear in this poem that by this time she was growing weary of the limitations of the slam and desiring to push the boundaries of the form in radical ways. As evidence of this, "I Don't Want to Slam" is longer than the allowed time limit for a slam poem. Second, it lacks her characteristic power, fierceness, rhyming skills, and overtly political critique of hegemony. And that is the craftiness of the piece: that she critiques, from the inside out, the very institution that brought her notoriety and a platform to advocate for the oppressed globally.

Chin intentionally disrupts the organization of the slam, using its rules as a weapon against it. NPS competitions allow individual slammers only three minutes to perform a poem. If the slammer goes over time, they are disqualified. During the final round of the 2000 NPS, Chin intentionally went over her time at the risk of isolating herself from her teammates and the then-growing slam community in general. For Chin, words are powerful and can potentially bypass the time limit of a slam competition, as well as the expectations of how a slam poet looks, sounds, and performs. In a 2004 essay, "Almost Famous," Chin recalls her experience as a "Def Poet" on the HBO series *Russell Simmons's Def Poetry Jam* and the subsequent Broadway production. She reports that aspects of her lifestyle changed with the success of the Broadway show: She had a reliable source of income, and she was more visible. Conversely, she recalls the stress, guilt, and all-consuming nature of performing eight shows a week. During the run, she became concerned about maintaining her artistic sensibility and signature performance style while working within a commercial machine that was turning the slam into a popular form.[49]

The freedom (and freeing effect) of solo art is best articulated by Jill Dolan, who has called slam poetry a site of "utopia in performance": "small but profound moments in which performance calls the attention of the audience in a way that lifts everyone slightly above the present, into a hopeful feeling of what the world might be like if every moment of our lives were as emotionally voluminous, generous, aesthetically striking, and intersubjectively intense."[50] Javon Johnson agrees that these "moments of hope" happen on stage but that

48. Chin, "I Don't Want to Slam," 208.

49. Chin does not suggest that the "media"—television, film, radio, or the commercial stage—dilutes the explicit content, direct message, and immediacy of spoken word.

50. Dolan, *Utopia in Performance*, 5.

within slam communities "those moments are marked and marred by racism, sexism, homophobia, classism, and a host of other troubling community practices" that are far from ideal.[51] Therefore, while Chin's and others' intersectional approach to slam poetry influences social awareness, instills hope, and encourages social change, oppressive systems can find their way into slam communities and, as Johnson argues, those moments should be addressed and corrected to ensure equity on the stage and behind the scenes.

Crossfire, MotherStruck!, and Kindred on the Rock

The second and third decades of Chin's career mark both life-altering changes, including motherhood, and a surge of creative productivity. In 2012 Chin gave birth to a daughter she named Zuri, a life event that shifted her perspective on the significance of mortality and her body of work—"I immediately began obsessing about death and performance and legacy and heritage."[52] The deaths of playwrights Derek Walcott and ntozake shange, she confesses, led her to a newfound desire to archive her poetry and prose. Instituting her work via publication is in itself a lovin' on act. Valuing her own contributions as an artist worthy of the tangibility and accessibility of live performance, recorded performance, and the printed word signifies a trifold embrace of herself as a performance artist whose work has the potential to impact the world well beyond her lifespan.

In 2019 Chin published her first collection of poems, *Crossfire: A Litany for Survival,* which received a 2020 American Book Award. On why it took her nearly three decades to publish a book of poetry, she explains that as a Black person in Jamaica, a country colonized by the British, she assumed a postcolonial mentality that she had nothing substantive or of quality to publish. She recalls her experience under the mentorship of poet and playwright Derek Walcott, who praised her writing—having invited her to study with him at Boston University for six months—but found the subject matter—her vagina, orgasms, feminist politics, and lesbianism—to be niche and, largely, uninteresting to others outside of Black lesbian-feminist and womanist circles.[53] Candidly, she explains, "I didn't know how to write without centering my politics, my identity as a lesbian and a woman, my female body, and how it made me vulnerable in a world dictated by the desires and rules of cisgender

51. J. Johnson, *Killing Poetry,* 81.
52. J. Johnson, *Killing Poetry,* 81.
53. See LeBlanc, "Staceyann Chin on Why."

men."[54] And not knowing how to write for the dominant readership kept Chin from publishing her writing for a wider audience. Again, the messaging that women artists receive about their work is often filtered through ideologies and aesthetic expectations that seek to silence the female voice and woman's perspective, or, at the very least, correct them, put them on the straight and narrow, so they can assimilate to the dominant culture's assumptions of what a "good girl" should think, write, and perform.

Prior to the publication of *Crossfire,* her 2015 solo play, *MotherStruck!*, opened at the Lynn Redgrave Theater at Culture Project in New York City, under the direction of Cynthia Nixon. A New York Times Critics Pick, the play was reviewed by Charles Isherwood, who praised Chin's "magnetic presence" and indefatigable performance.[55] Isherwood gives a fair, largely positive critique, observing that "Ms. Chin's easygoing radiance helps keep you hooked, even when the writing grows slightly slack. And certainly her story has plenty of hairpin curves and alarming surprises—no shortage of drama, in short."[56] She has perfected that ability to find the drama in a story since her slam poetry days. Watching the highs and lows of her fight for motherhood in *MotherStruck!* means watching Chin's earnest and funny vacillations between anxiety and ecstasy and back to, ultimately, a state of contentment as the mother of one. The play opens with Chin reflecting on her fear of becoming pregnant as a young girl because of her aunt's early fear-based teachings including a "you better not get pregnant" directive and the subsequent terror that remained with her even into adulthood. During puberty, simply being a girl can become a "problem" for a child, especially developing Black girls. Their girlhoods are truncated because they are charged with making preventative decisions about adult concerns like sex and reproduction with little-to-no sexual health knowledge or education. Fear is meant to keep them from having sex, but fear can, inadvertently, keep them from progressing normally as autonomous sexual beings. In an effort to "protect" Black girls, fear-based sexual education can sully their nascent relationship with their bodies, with sex, and with the notion of parenthood. In the play, Chin reckons with the scarring messaging of her youth while pursuing single motherhood in the urban city.

MotherStruck! toured off and on between 2015 and 2020, with stops in Chicago, Illinois, at the Greenhouse Theater Center (directed by Ron Russell); Washington, DC, at Studio Theatre (directed by Matt Torney); and Providence, Rhode Island at Brown University. Later adapted into an independent television series, the seventy-five-minute play "is about [Chin's] 'collision'

54. Chin, *Crossfire,* 3.
55. Isherwood, "Review," 1.
56. Isherwood, "Review," 1.

into motherhood alongside the story of [her] upbringing: the absence of her mother, the issues that came with being raised by a strict puritanical aunt, and her own desires and fears around motherhood as a person who was not mothered herself."[57] The latter issue of not being mothered is substantial for her. Many un(der)mothered girls and women question whether they will be good mothers, whether they become mothers through conception, adoption, or what Hill Collins terms "othermothering." Additionally, Chin discloses that trying to conceive as a Black queer person can be a logistical, biological, and practical nightmare. In her search for answers throughout her "dramatic pregnancy quest" as a "geriatric mother," she finds a dearth of information available for lesbians who want to become pregnant.[58] When asked by an interviewer for *The Atlantic* why she was performing an autobiographical work about her "route to family," Chin responds:

> There are so few stories about women who do not live in the lap of luxury. Who may be artists or lesbians or, y'know, immigrants, whatever, who want to become parents. And it's not a straight path. Y'know, we're not, I'm not going to marry someone and we're gonna get together and have a baby together. I mean that's not what happened with me. So, you know, there's this other route to family that I discovered.[59]

Here, she articulates the challenges of queer parenthood as a woman of advanced age who wants to conceive, carry, and give birth to a child. There are considerations that same-gender-loving women, let alone single lesbians, have to consider in order to make families "the old fashioned way," and even though Chin became pregnant and gave birth to her child at the age of thirty nine, she experienced heavy bleeding due to fibroids that were not discovered until she was pregnant, causing her to spend the majority of her pregnancy on bed rest. *MotherStruck!* is an archive of an event in Chin's life that has further shaped her progressive perspective on women's reproductive rights and bodily autonomy.

Laura Collins-Hughes of *The New York Times* reports that, since the birth of her child, Chin is as political as ever—she is still pro-abortion (even more so), she is still a progressive feminist, and she is still a proud Black lesbian. Nothing has changed much except for her capacity to love another human. Of Chin and her daughter's relationship, Collins-Hughes writes, "They talk a lot, she and Zuri, and Ms. Chin is raising her daughter to think for herself and

57. Reddy, "Saints We Call Upon,"1.

58. See FORA.tv, "Staceyann Chin and Cynthia Nixon."

59. See FORA.tv, "Staceyann Chin and Cynthia Nixon."

speak her mind—even if, as happened the other day, that means a tiny girl voicing displeasure at her mother's use of a certain explicative."[60] Chin and Zuri converse without the expectation that a child should speak when spoken to, an experience that Chin was subjected to as a child. The elder Chin's radical feminist approach to childrearing is most evident in their living room protests (LRPs). They began filming these short videos together in their Brooklyn home and regularly uploading them to Chin's YouTube page in 2014 when Zuri was two years old. In 2021 they filmed an LRP together in which they discussed the concept of home and practice of homemaking. Zuri, seven years old at the time, observes that together they are a nomadic family—they were in Jamaica for what was to be only a year at the time of filming, presumably due to the COVID-19 pandemic and its impact on New York City—while voicing a fluid understanding of home that includes both Brooklyn and Jamaica.[61]

In 2022 Chin opened the doors to Kindred on the Rock—a seventy-acre farm "for artists, activists & freedom-lovers building community & seeking freedom"—in Point Hill, Jamaica. Replete with goats and chickens, the farm, which she purchased during the pandemic, is Chin's latest arts-activist project. It is a recess of sorts that, at present, can house over a dozen people for weekend retreats, among other collective events. Yet this time, she is not alone. With Zuri and her international friends, she is making a communal space with a community of rebellious artists, activists, allies, and scholars in a Jamaica that, Chin has observed, has changed for the better in terms of its tolerance of queer people. Ever invested in utopian ideas, Chin writes, "I'm always looking for my true path, even [if] it means following that narrow dirt road running along the lines of irrational hope in my palm. I was never meant to have money, but I am not destined to starve either. So my hands remain open."[62] In addition to negotiating the intricacies of home and homemaking, Chin engages in an ethics of reflection as she facilitates the day-to-day responsibilities of Kindred. "How do you own something and make it a community space?" she ponders, in conversation with actress Diane Neal.[63] In a grassroots effort to undo rigid hierarchies of class in Jamaica while contributing meaningfully to her many communities, Chin's work with Kindred is a socialist experiment in diplomacy whose outcome is to be determined.

Whether laboring on the farm; recording and uploading antiracist, antihomophobic, antisexist, anticlassist, antifascist, and antiestablishment poems to her social media accounts or giving international public talks and lectures,

60. Collins-Hughes, "Staceyann Chin Worries About Money," 1.

61. Chin, "#LivingRoomProtest #81."

62. Chin, "Life tumbles on at @kindredontherock . . ."

63. Hear Say Diane Neal, "WE'RE GOING TO JAMAICA."

Chin is still hopeful that her art and activism will transform perspectives, dismantle oppression, and more accurately represent the marginalized. She continues to stand barefoot on stages speaking unadulterated truths centered in the core beliefs she formed in Jamaica then fleshed out and reconfigured in the US. Characteristic of a lifelong pursuit of corporeal, spiritual, and artistic freedom, she invites others to make a new world with her on and off stage. In the face of oppressive systems that deem her other, incomprehensible, and without value, Chin claims space for her body and narratives in the theater, on screen, on the farm, and in the city. Through intense acts of lovin' on herself and others since she was a girl, she remains in process, feeling, finding, and making home where the Caribbean and the United States meet.

AFTERWORD

Recovery Efforts

In an enlightening forum discussion with theater artists, dramaturgs, and scholars, Isaiah Matthew Wooden opens with a statement that summarizes the inherent stakes of making, teaching, and critiquing Black theater. He writes: "Black theater is always under pressure—to entertain, to challenge, to inform, to provoke, to represent, among other things. Correspondingly, Black theater artists often come to know and understand pressure quite intimately."[1] The pressure Wooden writes of stems from the limited opportunities that Black artists have to present their art, especially in the US, where race, gender, sexuality, class, and citizenship increasingly determine one's right to think, speak, write, and act as an American. Because Black people's citizenship has been contested since they were brought here, the pressure cooker for Black theater practitioners and scholars has an inarticulable intensity. There is always a sense that one must get "it" right, if "it" is the Black or American or woman or queer experience.

Because of such pressures, some Black queer playwrights intentionally subvert the notion of the single Black queer experience and, instead, choose to explore the possible, not necessarily plausible, experiential possibilities. Consider Jeremy O. Harris's *Slave Play* (2019), for example, which has captivated

1. Carpenter et al., "Black Theater, Under Pressure," 7.

and challenged audiences by reconfiguring historical narratives in which race, gender, sexuality, and notions of power and play collide and, at times, clash in ways that at once excite and distance audiences from the rigidity of histories they hold dear. With this book, I hope to have demonstrated that such provocations are not new in Black performance, and that Black queer feminist performance artists (and scholars), in particular, have been doing this kind of work out loud and under the cover of night while under pressure to document Black queer experiences in all of their varied presentations.

As Khalid Y. Long rightly asserts, in the same forum, "There is still a need for more Black queer visibility on the stage (and in critical studies)."[2] Furthermore, he convincingly argues that this effort to illuminate Black queer experience on stages and pages "is not the sole responsibility of queer artists," calling us (practitioners and scholars) "to apply pressure on straight, cisgender artists to take up the mantle and create fully developed characters that are queer, gender nonbinary, trans-identified, and others who are socially alienated as it relates to their gender and sexuality."[3] This leads me to recognize interventions, or what I refer to as *recovery efforts,* to mitigate the absence of authentic and varied queer-of-color stories in theater and performance work, which I am primarily attempting to do with this book. I have also been in the presence of recovery efforts by playwrights and directors who may or may not identify as Black, queer, or woman, yet are clearly curious in their imaginings of Blackness and queerness. They are getting into what John Lewis called "good trouble," I think, in their artistic explorations and interrogations of the lives and worlds of characters whose identities (perceived and self-defined) traverse an increasingly complex range.

Lovin' on in the works of Holmes, Bridgforth, Chin, Grays, and Rees covers romantic, sexual, spiritual, familial, national, and other relationships endemic to the human experience, in order to evince the depths of the impact of the internal storms that their queer characters contend with along their Odyssean journeys to personhood, freedom, and survival. *A Conditional Embrace* is an exhumation of a modicum of works by Black queer women artists—many of whom have had limited space and opportunity to present their work to audiences on commercial stages and screens or in publications—although that long-standing trend has shown some improvement. With this project, I have demonstrated that Black queer feminist performance, as an aesthetic, allows multiply situated persons to articulate the specificity of their lives with and against existing identitarian terms and ideas. Artists of the

2. Carpenter et al., "Black Theater, Under Pressure," 23.
3. Carpenter et al., "Black Theater, Under Pressure," 23.

genre and style inform audiences about how it feels in their bodies to straddle identitarian fences while juggling communal allegiances. They write of the weight of economic, societal, and political storms they weather to squeeze themselves into reductive categories that temporarily provide shelter but never quite qualify as home. In the tradition of Black women's narratives, hope is the catalyst for reconfigurations of home through declarations of pride and demonstrations of love.

A Conditional Embrace is not meant to be an exhaustive survey of Black queer feminist performance; it could never be. By analyzing the works of a handful of innovative artists working in the twentieth and twenty-first centuries, I have highlighted flexible blueprints that are inspired by and have inspired the work of BQFP artists. Holmes, Bridgforth, Grays, Rees, and Chin make space for Black lesbian identity in their plays and performance pieces, claiming previously prohibited geographies to represent the diversity and nuance of Black lesbian life. These and other texts and performances are viable art pieces that deserve (1) to be critically analyzed and theorized, (2) to be produced at large theaters, and (3) to be published in theater and performance anthologies. While playwrights and performers are creating new Black queer feminist works for generally receptive audiences, without critical attention, these works, like so many in the past, will be overlooked.

BQFP artists create viable homes and worlds for their characters through performative acts that lead Black lesbians closer to home. Each artist depicts homemaking in the following ways: (1) They reclaim spaces that have historically been unwelcoming to those who appear and identify as Black, woman, and/or lesbian; (2) they revise history by inserting Black lesbian narratives where they have been absent; and (3) they deconstruct negative stereotypes associated with Black lesbian womanhood. Although the artists depict different aspects of homemaking and community-building, each presents or represents such characters in the midst of productive and reproductive processes that not only allow them to carve out and shape their own identities, but also permit diverse audiences to witness acts of lovin' on that lead to some material, emotional, and physical satisfaction for the protagonist. Again, lovin' on is an effort, an act, an attempt toward righting wrongs that deny oppressed people the right to life, liberty, and the pursuit of happiness. In that way, acts of lovin' on are a means to a utopic end. But as the works studied in this book make clear, lovin' on oneself and somebody else is far from that end; it is the work required to reach it.

With the variations of identities center stage in BQFP, the genre explicitly and unapologetically sets its compass toward narratives in which women characters self-define in intersectional terms and love on other women freely.

Through intergenerational transfers of knowledge, BQFP artists reconfigure tired, recycled stereotypes of Black womanhood while exposing overlapping systems of oppression that impact the livability of Black women, generally, and Black queer women, specifically. Through deep explorations of unwritten policies of membership that cause dis-ease within marginalized communities, the artists examine the ways in which Black queer people work around/through that dis-ease by challenging notions of membership and belonging. Last, they emphasize the importance of love and the various ways in which it, in all its forms, is an act of resistance within and outside of those communities.

Literary storms are not unlike the literal storms of life—those that govern our personal and public, individual and communal, and creative and intellectual realities. They are sure to come, no matter how quiet you are and no matter where you hide, as is evident in the stories of outliers who weather societal pressures to conform in ways that suit the greater majority. As I have shown, those on the periphery of society, those who have secrets they are afraid to tell, and those who are loud and proud about who they are and how they are can recover from traumas inflicted by well-meaning and cruel factions that misrecognize them as broken, inept, and unfit. The beaten, battered, and bruised can emerge victorious. They can recover and piece themselves back together. One cannot do that, however, without a sense of pride and a reliable support system.

In the theater and on screen, scenes depicting Black women's resistance to oppression (storms) tend to ignite fires in those who see themselves reflected. They also inspire other marginalized voices to add their perspectives to the discourse on race, gender, and sexuality in creative ways. At their bravest, these artists depict women's bodies as sites of homemaking, and through sexual intimacy, queer kinship, and familial connection, their characters manage to reconnect with the colonized bodies of their foremothers. In the pursuit of recovering truths that have been lost, shushed, and unspoken, they gift narratives to publics in hopes that they might reach back to meet them where they are. But storms—big and small, literal and literary—give and take.

In 2020 yet another storm threatened the lives of global citizens. The COVID-19 pandemic brought worldwide industries, especially those in which liveness is key, to a sudden halt. With the reopening of theater and performance spaces in 2021 and 2022, conscious decision-making and difficult conversations were happening around which plays should be included in a modern American production season. Kendra Capece and Patrick Scorese observe, "The breakdown of the art/performance and protest/struggle binaries intersects in the work emerging from the pandemic. The lines between art and activism have always been blurred, but the current crisis has necessitated new ways to create and engage with art and others."[4] With the public outrage over the murders of George Floyd, Ahmaud Arbery, and Breonna Taylor, to name just a few, along with global isolation during the pandemic, there was time and interest in having conversations about what American theater might be when the world reopened. In the aftermath, some theater companies began funding projects that aligned with their mission to produce more diverse works. Some revisited queer-of-color plays and commissioned new works.

From 2022 to 2024, Pillsbury House + Theatre in Minneapolis produced a series of Sharon Bridgforth's performance works, including *The bull-jean Experience, the bull-jean stories,* and *bull-jean/we wake.*[5] Celebrating Bridgforth's novel with a two-year long exploration of the original text, a multimedia adaptation, and a follow-up novel is a clear sign that bull-jean has had a significant impact on a generation or more of Black queer folks and allies. In 2023 Steppenwolf Theatre Company produced Donnetta Lavinia Grays's *Last Night and the Night Before,* which premiered in 2019 at Denver Center for the Arts—both of which were directed by Valerie Curtis-Newton. In the play, Rachel's and Nadima's lives are upended when Rachel's drug-addicted sister, Monica, and her ten-year-old daughter, Samantha, arrive at their doorstep in Brooklyn from the fictional town of Vixten, Georgia. The couple's relationship is normalized; they do not love in secret. The secret is, instead, embedded in the mystery surrounding Monica and Samantha, who are running away from something (or someone) down South. In the playwright's notes, Grays clearly outlines the queer characters in order to reduce the likelihood of stereotypical performances. When a character's sexuality or gender expression extends beyond the heteronormative, unfortunately, there is a risk of misinterpretation. She instructs, "Rachel and Nadima are lesbians. Simply and affirmatively. They exist in both feminine and masculine space fluidly. Resist any impulse to emulate a heteronormative relationship or define them through a heteronormative gaze. Allow their love to be complex."[6] Articulating her intent allows her to preempt heterocentric readings of the play, especially by those who are not "in the life" or are more apt to execute an outdated vision of a lesbian relationship.

4. Capece and Scorese, *Pandemic Performance,* 9.

5. *The bull-jean Experience,* performed by Omi Osun Joni L. Jones with visual art by Za'Nia Coleman, was produced in 2022; *the bull-jean stories* was produced in 2023, starring Aimee K. Bryant, under the direction of Signe V. Harriday; and in 2024 *bull-jean/we wake,* starring Jones and Bryant, was directed by Daniel Alexander Jones—all at Pillsbury House + Theatre.

6. Grays, *Last Night and the Night Before,* iv.

In 2022 Soho Rep produced South Korean playwright Hansol Jung's dramedy *Wolf Play.* Ash and Robin, a queer interracial couple, adopt a Korean boy, Genu, who is presented as a puppet operated by an actor, yet perceived as a human boy in the world of the play. Jung investigates the ethics of transnational and cross-cultural adoption in this *Peter and the Wolf*–inspired story while illuminating the challenges and labor involved in cross-cultural communications and childrearing. Ash, a Black queer nonbinary person, played memorably by Esco Jouléy, is a boxer who is noticeably distant toward Genu initially.[7] Later, at the expense of their boxing training, Ash becomes the only person the scared child connects with. Ash's race and queer gender identity complicate a compound adoption narrative and invite us to question the idea of the modern American family.

Another example is Katori Hall's Pulitzer Prize–winning comedy, *The Hot Wing King.* In 2023 I attended a production of the play, directed by Hall, at the Alliance Theatre in Atlanta, Georgia. It was apparent, as the play progressed, that every time the central gay couple (Cordell and Dwayne) touched or kissed, which they did often, a small group of young Black men in the audience would laugh, talk, and scoff. While I was annoyed at their disruption, I was happy that these young men, and all who bore witness during its run, got to experience a story of a Black (queer) family in the theater. *It is a start, and something like progress.* To be fair, the young men were probably not expecting this play to feature so many queer characters at the center of the story which, considering the history of homophobia in Black communities, may have contributed to their shock and awe. Considering Hall's unapologetic inclusion of queer characters on the popular show *P Valley*—an episodic adaptation of her 2015 play, *Pussy Valley,* which conceivably drew audiences to what was, on the day I attended, a packed theater—I am unsure what kind of story they were expecting to see.

The stage is not a screen. It is live. It is intimate. It is immediate. And the audience can talk back in ways that shift the energy in the room for good or bad. The audience can embrace what they see on the stage. Or not. The more public the displays of affection between Cordell and Dwayne (kissing, holding hands, hugging), for example, the more uneasy the young men became. They did not disrupt to the point of being removed from the theater, but many heads in the balcony turned toward them and they were shushed several times. "Uncomfortable" is the best word to describe others of us in the audience during these few but distracting moments. The best phrase to describe the young men, however, is "big mad." While there is much to be said about

7. In March 2023 I had the pleasure of attending a Sunday matinee of *Wolf Play* at MCC.

discomfort at the theater, what interests me more is the practice of an ethics of love that involves restraint and listening on the part of all involved (the lovers and the haters), especially in an instance like this one, in which there was an obvious intracultural clash in an intimate setting of mostly Black people (on stage and off).

A Southern Black woman playwright, Hall audaciously crafts a play in which the majority of the Black characters from Memphis, Tennessee, exist along the spectrum of queerness, and she makes no apology for it. Hall's statement with the play is, as I understand it, that this is Black community and these men and gender-nonconforming folks are Black folks, too. With *Hot Wing King,* Hall draws spectator-participants in without prefacing that "This is a queer play" or "This is a Black play." It is *all* of that. It is also a play about family. By the end of the performance, the majority of the audience stood to their feet, applauding. Like Virginia Grise, after seeing *the bull-jean stories* in the 1990s in a theater in Austin, Texas, I thought and said aloud with newfound excitement after the curtain fell in one of the most influential regional theaters in Georgia, "How Black, feminist, queer, and damned Southern of Hall." And this while Luther Vandross's driving "Never Too Much" played over the sound system.

Centering this song in a scene during the play, and then replaying it post play as an audience sendoff, Hall pays homage to the late rhythm-and-blues music icon and puts Vandross in conversation with Black queer experience and performance. Dawn Porter's 2024 documentary, *Luther: Never Too Much,* is a musical exposé and a recovery effort of the Manhattan-born crooner, who was notoriously private about his personal life but is widely suspected to have been gay. In a 1992 interview with John Tesh, Vandross divulges, "I'm still looking for that meaningful other person in my life. That is something that baffles me, that I haven't been able to find. And it seems like such a basic thing."[8] What is interesting about this revelation is not the singer's skillful omission of pronouns to denote the gender of his desired love subject, nor is it that he is discursively searching for the root cause of the absence of such a person in his life, but that he longs for that someone. He longs for a lover of consequence.

Porter uncovers then lingers on the topic of the absence of love in Vandross's life. The director features a clip of him during a 1991 interview on *The Oprah Winfrey Show* which finds him responding to a question whose answer is eye-opening but not fully legible to an early nineties audience, for which deep discussions of sexuality were still taboo. When a woman in the audience

8. See Gaspin, *One on One with John Tesh.*

asks what his favorite original song to sing is, Vandross says, "'Any Love' remains my favorite song. [*inhales*] Because it is probably the only real autobiographical song that I wrote. That was exactly the way I was feeling when I wrote the song." Many singer-songwriters write from an autobiographical perspective; therefore, it is noteworthy that this one song is, at this point in his decades-long career, the truest and most personal. Vandross's words and embodiment here are telling. Notice that he inhales audibly, giving himself a beat to choose his words carefully, only to reveal just enough but never too much. The lyrics to the mid-tempo song are testimonial and introspective when one understands how deep and winding queer closets can be the longer they are kept closed. In the song, he reflects on how he occasionally talks to himself, reminding himself to be grateful for the abundance he has but, like Gloria Carter in "Smile," there is a part of him that is imprisoned, screaming to be seen, heard, and felt.

Silenced (or shushed) people tend to reveal their truths in unexpected, often methodical, ways. Vandross notoriously and purposely avoided gendering the subject of his desire when discussing his love songs and love life in interviews. In fact, he wrote and co-wrote many songs that take a gender-neutral position, which likely made singing them for audiences of varied sexualities and belief systems an easier and more lucrative effort. But one can only hide their true desires for so long. Vandross obfuscates the particularities of love and desire in the lyrics of his songs. Thus, when the cast of *The Hot Wing King* breaks the fourth wall in a singalong of "Never Too Much"—an up-tempo song popular at African American cultural events, such as cookouts, weddings, and baby showers—the audience (even those uncomfortable with the play's queerness) is compelled to participate; they need no invitation. Through this subtle gesture of appreciation, Vandross, a Black man who may or may not have been gay, is given center stage and yet another moment to peek out of the closet. Considering the dichotomy between the Black community's embrace of his talent as a singer, writer, and producer and the secret that dare not speak its name, Vandross, the man and the lover, remains a mystery to a public that considers him family. We love on him in death as we did in life, although we never *really* knew him. Most who knew him personally protect his legacy by refraining from speaking definitively about his personal life. That's love. It is also love to wish we could have known more about our beloved, more about our "sweeter" kinfolk.

Through recovery efforts in Black performance, we call back to the past to extend "any love" to those who have shaped and contributed to the culture yet received a conditional embrace in the times and spaces in which they made their contributions. This communal work, I believe, is how culture is built and sustained over time. Despite ongoing attempts to negate and erase the histories of marginalized people, and despite the existing gaps in our foundational histories, those stories can and should be documented. Without such efforts, they will surely be lost to the social, economic, and political storms that challenge love in all its representations. But I am as hopeful as ever because the works of those writing in a Black queer feminist aesthetic instruct me to hope for an expansive, inclusive, equal, and diverse future that makes room for people, no matter their race, class, gender, sexuality, nationality, or citizenship status. As Mother Nature continues to demonstrate, when storms roll in, no one is safe. One can only hope that when the heavy winds and rain are upon you, there will be someone close by to help you rebuild.

•

The storms that pass through the South can be treacherous. When I was a child, I had no fear of a tree falling on our house, of the power going out (*that* was inevitable), or that my family might be carried away altogether by high winds. We regularly evacuated our town and headed north to safety at least once a year during hurricane season. The times we did not leave, an elder, often my grandmother, would tell us kids, "Shhh! Get quiet! A storm's coming," the significance of which we neither understood nor cared about. *Storms always came.* Like the elder folk before her, my grandmother believed that the thunder and lightning represented the "devil beating his wife"—at least, that was the script she recited to scare us wired children into keeping quiet and to settle her own rising anxieties as thunder cracked and lightning painted the sky.

Children believe what adults tell them, and even if they doubt the veracity of their tales, they learn to accept uttered myths without question. At that young age, I recognized the intent behind her commandment; it always felt well-meaning. And children know the difference between care and cruelty. Her guidance was the way she loved on us, along with hugs (she called them "sugar") that could squeeze the life out of a little body. Her stern direction to "Get quiet!" was one of the ways she knew to protect her family from that type of storm. Other storms came, however, storms insidious enough to rip apart our family unit, and she managed those, too—often through the use and encouragement of silence, which has its benefits. It also has consequences. It is true that keeping quiet can keep one alive and alert in the midst of a storm. It can also prevent one from living fully and completely out of fear that the ways in which they do will disrupt the status quo.

ACKNOWLEDGMENTS

When I began preliminary research for this project in 2011, I never would have thought I would still be as passionate and inspired by the depth, breadth, and beauty of the artists and their works. Yet, I am still. To Shirlene, Sharon, Staceyann, Donnetta, and Dee: your presentations and representations of the complexities of hope through animated acts of love exceed the boundaries of theater and cinema's traditional applications. Thank you for speaking and writing when silence was the safer choice. It is difficult to find the words to explain how important your works have been to girls and women like us. I hope this book contains those words.

This book would not be possible without the support of institutions and organizations including Vanderbilt University, the University of Georgia, the American Theatre and Drama Society (ATDS), the Association for Theatre in Higher Education (ATHE), Black Theatre Network (BTN), and the National Women's Studies Association (NWSA), who invested in my research by way of grants, fellowships, and research funding. These include a grant from ATDS and ATHE, and a Publication Subvention Grant and a Dean's Research Studio Grant from the College of Arts and Science at Vanderbilt University. A very special thank you to E. Patrick Johnson, Ana Jimenez-Moreno, the two external readers, Elizabeth Zaleski, and The Ohio State University Press for believing in this project.

I am deeply indebted to Freda Scott Giles, Emily Sahakian, Mical R. Whitaker, Marla Carlson, and Patricia Del Rey for your scholarship and mentorship. Thank you to the many scholars, artists, thinkers, talkers, and activists who have shaped my thoughts on performance and performativity, many of whom are cited or referenced in this book with intentionality and gratitude. To those with whom I have worked closely through service, performance, and other endeavors, thank you for embracing my sameness and difference and for working gracefully around and through the obstacles that are bound to arise in our field.

Thank you to Juanita Johnson-Bailey, Beverly Guy-Sheftall, Paul K. Jackson, Michael Dinwiddie, David Z. Saltz, Faedra Chatard Carpenter, Ramón H. Rivera-Servera, José Esteban Muñoz, Mikell Pinkney, Eloise Robinson, Barbara McCaskill, Vivian Appler, Stuart J. Hecht, Ryan Claycomb, Detra Payne, Megan Minto Bromberg, Beth Turner, Billicia Hines, Melisa Cahnmann-Taylor, Martine Kei Green-Rogers, Nichole Ray, Djola Branner, Le'Mil Eiland, Betty Smith Franklin, Chris Eaket, Belen Calingacion, Patricia Richards, Persephone Felder-Fentress, Daniel Banks, Jennifer DeVere Brody, Jennifer-Scott Mobley, T. Chester, Tom Zhang, Maya Roth, Donatella Galella, Lundeana M. Thomas, Kimberly Jew, Brian E. Hererra, La Donna L. Forsgren, Isaiah Matthew Wooden, Kirsten Pullen, Kelly Happe, Heather Nathans, DeRon S. Williams, Terry Hatfield, Cecilia Herles, Lisa Biggs, Aoise Stratford, Jacqueline Springfield, Lynn Deboeck, Omiyemi (Artisia) Green, Omi Osun Joni L. Jones, Corey Roberts, Renée Charlow, Eunice Ferreira, Jill Dolan, Kareem Khubchandani, and Sara Warner for your knowledge, guidance, and encouragement. Thank you to Leah Lowe, Phillip Frank, Christin Essin, Ibby Cizmar, Kevin Murphy, Wilna J. Taylor, Krista Knight, Liz Haynes, Chezare A. Warren, Rebecca VanDiver, Hannah Chalman, Margaret Baldwin-Pendergrass, Dawn Eskridge, Angela Farr Schiller, Emily Kitchens, Amanda Wansa Morgan, Karen Robinson, Charlie Parrot, Nicole Adkins, Amelia Fischer, Kara Cantrell, Tim Ellis, Tom Fish, Jim Davis, Pamela Rodriguez-Montero, Brittany Johnson, Rebecca Makus, and Ming Chen—for your support, guidance, and/or collegiality.

To those acquaintances and contemporaries who have rooted for this project and pushed me to trust myself through the writing process, this work would be immaterial without you. Thank you to Brenda Porter, Alia Shakira, Tracey Graves, Aimee K. Bryant, Deidre Schoo, Brian Silcox, and the Shirlene Holmes Estate, whose enthusiasm fueled me to the finish line. Jieun Lee and Jamie Palmer-Asemota: thank you for accountability and unconditional friendship. Angela Chrishelle Hall: thank you for secrets, art, and sister-kinship. I miss everything about you. Khalid Y. Long: thank you for your brilliance, passion, friendship, and example. Daniel Alexander Jones: thank you for your support, light, and innovative vision.

To my students, thank you for the lessons taught and lessons learned. I am a more caring, focused, and intentional educator because of you. Kelly Berry: Thank you for the life-changing opportunity that could have only happened because of your forethought and leadership. You are missed beyond words. Pamela Bourland-Davis, a.k.a. "Dr. Pam": I have known you since I was nineteen years old working alongside my peers under the instruction and guidance of faculty, like the great Mical Whitaker, Gary and Brenda Dartt, Kelly Berry, James Harbour, Rebecca Kennerly, Dana Harrell, and Belen Calingacion. You normalized making lemonade out of lemons as we experimented with all forms of performance in an oversized trailer with classrooms and a small black-box that leaked when it rained yet was a home to theater kids who made memories and magic there year after year. You led from a place of abundance and taught me what leadership can and should be. Thank you. Sleep softly.

To Helen, Ella, and Rosie, for your love and faith that I will always come home to you. Thank you for your distraction and understanding when I shut myself away in my office thinking, typing, and singing away. To my parents, Charles and Deidré Tift, and grandparents, Jesse and Rosa Tift and Hardie and Eleanor Cobb, for teaching me the value of education and pride in self and community. To my brothers, K.D. and Kehri, for your love and support. Being raised with you made me strong and soft in all the ways I need to exist in this world. To my family: I received every story you told and those you did not *have* to tell. I am grateful for your sacrifice. The lessons you taught me color my life in the most beautiful shades.

Writing this book, I found myself navigating the gamut of human experiences that the characters in the theater works and films discussed herein navigate, and, honestly, these stories helped me to find the silver linings in my storms; they helped me see the "rainbow after the rain" that Lena tells Ruth about with wonder at her man-child's transformation in the final act of Lorraine Hansberry's *A Raisin in the Sun.* The human experience of "growing up" and "into" oneself through pursuits of personhood, freedom, friendship, profession, partnership, parenthood, and community-building have their challenges—you lose people, places, and things along the way—but those challenges build strong foundations, character, and a resoluteness that only hard work and harder times catalyze. There are few human experiences that have not been documented in literature, theater, film, and performance in some time, place, and form. It gives me solace, most days, to know that when I think I am alone in any experience, I can turn to art and find it on a page, stage, or screen. May the work continue.

APPENDIX

Musical Notes

I am a lifelong lover of music, and while writing, I had music playing in my headphones or through my studio monitors. As a result, there is music in the pages of this book—much of which lyrically engages with notions of love acts and their material implications. The albums and songs that nudged me out of my head and into my body as I worked through the ideas, theories, and concepts that moved this study forward include those on this very short list: Stevie Wonder's *Innervisions* and *Songs in the Key of Life*; Kendrick Lamar's *GNX*; Brandy's *B7*; Bonnie Raitt's *Luck of the Draw*; H.E.R.'s *H.E.R.*; Tank's *Now or Never*; Migos's *Culture II*; Maxwell's *blackSUMMERS'night*; Yebba's *Dawn*; Jay-Z's *4:44*; Jazmine Sullivan's *Heaux Tales* and *Reality Show*; Sade's *Lover's Rock*; Liz Wright's *Salt*; Mario's *Dancing Shadows* and *Glad You Came*; Jidenna's *ME YOU & GOD*; Jojo's *tryin' not to think about it* and *good to know*; Zacardi Cortez's "Lord Do It For Me"; Beyoncé's *Renaissance*; and Robin Thicke's *Love After War* and "Put Your Lovin' On Me." These sonic gifts stimulated and informed my work as only art can do, inspiring the dialectics of love and pain that permeate each chapter.

BIBLIOGRAPHY

Adeyemi, Kemi. *Feels Right: Black Queer Women and the Politics of Partying in Chicago*. Duke University Press, 2022.

Alexander, M. Jacqui. *Pedagogies of Crossing: Meditations on Feminism, Sexual Politics, Memory, and the Sacred*. Duke University Press, 2005.

Anderson, Lisa M. *Black Feminism in Contemporary Drama*. University of Illinois Press, 2008.

Aptowicz, Cristin O'Keefe. *Words in Your Face: A Guided Tour Through Twenty Years of the New York City Poetry Slam*. Soft Skull Press, 2008.

Auslander, Philip. *Liveness: Performance in a Mediatized Culture*. 3rd ed. Routledge, 2022. https://doi.org/10.4324/9781003031314.

Avilez, GerShun. "Movement in Black: Queer Bodies and the Desire for Spatial Justice." In *Black Queer Freedom: Spaces of Injury and Paths of Desire*, 21–53. University of Illinois Press, 2020.

Baker, Christina N. "Rebellious Love: *Middle of Nowhere* and *Pariah*." In *Contemporary Black Women Filmmakers and the Art of Resistance*, 125–53. The Ohio State University Press, 2018.

Banks, Daniel. "The Hip Hop Theatre Initiative: We the Griot." In *Black Acting Methods: Critical Approaches*, 139–67. Routledge Press, 2016.

Banks, Daniel. *Say Word! Voices from Hip Hop Theater: An Anthology*. University of Michigan Press, 2011.

Beauboeuf-Lafontant, Tamara. *Behind the Mask of the Strong Black Woman: Voice and the Embodiment of a Costly Performance*. Temple University Press, 2009.

Bennett, Brit. *The Vanishing Half*. Riverhead Books, 2020.

Bogan, Lucille. "Lucille Bogan—B.D. Woman's Blues." In *Mouths of Rain: An Anthology of Black Lesbian Thought*, edited by Briona Simone Jones, 19. New Press, 2021.

Bogus, SDiane. "The Myth and Tradition of the Black Bulldagger." In *Mouths of Rain: An Anthology of Black Lesbian Thought*, edited by Briona Simone Jones, 287–93. New Press, 2021.

Brack, Charles Bennett, dir. *Dreams Deferred: The Sakia Gunn Film Project.* Third World Newsreel, 2008. https://video.alexanderstreet.com/watch/dreams-deferred-the-sakia-gunn-film-project.

Bratton, Elegance, dir. *Pier Kids.* PBS, 2021.

Bridgforth, Sharon. *blood pudding.* Unpublished manuscript, 1998. Available at New Dramatists, New York.

Bridgforth, Sharon. *bull-jean & dem/dey back.* 53rd State Press, 2022.

Bridgforth, Sharon. *the bull-jean stories.* RedBone Press, 1998.

Bridgforth, Sharon. *delta dandi.* In *solo/black/woman: scripts, interviews, and essays,* edited by E. Patrick Johnson and Ramón H. Rivera-Servera, 185–226. Northwestern University Press, 2014.

Bridgforth, Sharon. "a wo'mn called sir." *Deneuve: The Lesbian Magazine* 12, no. 4 (2002): 46.

Butler, Judith. *Gender Trouble: Feminism and the Subversion of Identity.* 2nd ed. Routledge, 1999.

Butler, Judith. "Introduction: Acting in Context." In *Undoing Gender,* 1–16. 2nd ed. Routledge, 2004.

Butler, Judith. "Precarious Life, Vulnerability, and the Ethics of Cohabitation." *Journal of Speculative Philosophy* 26, no. 2 (2012): 134–51.

Capece, Kendra, and Patrick Scorese, eds. *Pandemic Performance: Resilience, Liveness, and Protest in Quarantine Times.* Routledge, 2021.

Carpenter, Faedra Chatard, Soyica Diggs Colbert, Martine Kei Green-Rogers, et al. "Black Theater, Under Pressure." *Theater* 53, no. 1 (2023): 6–29. https://doi.org/10.1215/01610775-10226031.

Case, Sue-Ellen. "Towards a Butch-Femme Aesthetic." *Discourse* 11, no. 1 (1988): 55–73.

Cervenak, Sarah Jane. *Wandering: Philosophical Performances of Racial and Sexual Freedom.* Duke University Press, 2014.

Chadee, Derek, Chezelle Joseph, Claire Peters, Vandana Siew Sankar, Nisha Nair, and Jannel Philip. "Religiosity, and Attitudes Towards Homosexuals in a Caribbean Environment." *Social and Economic Studies* 62, no. 1 (2013): 1–28.

Chin, Staceyann. "2nd Annual Research Day." York College of Undergraduate Research at City University of New York. Filmed April 14, 2011. YouTube, http://youtu.be/ztYcVeGziog.com.

Chin, Staceyann. "Almost Famous." *Black Issues Book Review* 6, no. 2 (2004): 22–23. Literary Reference Center, EBSCO host.

Chin, Staceyann. "Coming Out to the Caribbean." In *does your mama know? An Anthology of Black Lesbian Coming Out Stories,* edited by Lisa C. Moore, 115–19. RedBone Press, 2009.

Chin, Staceyann. *Crossfire: A Litany for Survival.* Haymarket Books, 2019.

Chin, Staceyann. "I Don't Want to Slam." *Poetry Slam: The Competitive Art of Performance Poetry,* edited by Gary Mex Glazner, 206–9. Manic D Press, 2000.

Chin, Staceyann Chin. "Life tumbles on at @kindredontherock . . ." Posted February 24, 2023. Facebook, https://www.facebook.com/watch/?v=1056280899095891.

Chin, Staceyann. "#LivingRoomProtest #81: What Is Home?" Posted December 9, 2021. YouTube, https://www.youtube.com/watch?v=osOzBdfokXg&t=1s.

Chin, Staceyann. *The Other Side of Paradise: A Memoire.* Simon & Schuster, 2009.

Chin, Staceyann. "Staceyann Chin: Feminist or Womanist." Posted November 14, 2010. YouTube, https://www.youtube.com/watch?v=f9GiZZ4W5ho.

Chin, Staceyann. "Staceyann Chin: Poet for the People." In *Word Warriors: 35 Women Leaders in the Spoken Word Revolution,* edited by Alix Olson, 361–73. Seal Press, 2007.

Clarke, Cheryl L. "The Failure to Transform: Homophobia in the Black Community." In *Home Girls,* 2nd ed., 190–201. Kitchen Table Women of Color Press, 1983.

Clarke, Cheryl L. "Lesbianism: An Act of Resistance" (1981). In *This Bridge Called My Back: Writings by Radical Women of Color,* 4th ed., edited by Cherríe Moraga and Gloria Anzaldúa, 126–35. State University of New York Press, 2015.

Clift, Robert A. *Blacking Up: Hip-Hop's Remix of Race and Identity,* DVD (California Newsreel, 2010). https://video.alexanderstreet.com/watch/blacking-up-hip-hop-ṣ-remix-of-race-and-identity.

Coasten, Jane. "The Intersectionality Wars: When Kimberlé Crenshaw Coined the Term 30 Years Ago, It Was a Relatively Obscure Legal Concept. Then It Went Viral." *Vox,* May 28, 2019. https://www.vox.com/the-highlight/2019/5/20/18542843/intersectionality-conservatism-law-race-gender-discrimination.

Cohen, Cathy J. "Punks, Bulldaggers and Welfare Queens: The Radical Potential of Queer Politics?" In *Black Queer Studies: A Critical Anthology,* edited by E. Patrick Johnson and Mae G. Henderson, 21–51. Duke University Press, 2005.

Colbert, Soyica Diggs. *Black Movements: Performance and Cultural Politics.* Rutgers University Press, 2017. https://doi.org/10.36019/9780813588544.

Collins-Hughes, Laura. "Staceyann Chin Worries About Money, and Selling Out." *New York Times,* January 14, 2016. https://www.nytimes.com/2016/01/17/theater/staceyann-chin-worries-about-money-and-selling-out.html.

Craig, Traci, and Jessica LaCroix. "Tomboy as a Protective Identity." *Journal of Lesbian Studies* 15, no. 4 (2011): 450–65.

DeFrantz, Thomas F., and Anita Gonzalez, eds. *Black Performance Theory.* Duke University Press, 2014.

Dennie, Nneka D. *Mary Ann Shadd Cary.* Oxford University Press, 2024.

Derk, George. "Inverting Hollywood from the Outside In: The Films Within Cheryl Dunye's *The Watermelon Woman.*" *Screen* 59, no. 3 (2018): 293–310.

Diamond, Lisa M. *Sexual Fluidity: Understanding Women's Love and Desire.* Harvard University Press, 2008.

Dixon, Terence, dir. *Meeting the Man: James Baldwin in Paris.* Buzzy Enterprises, LTD, 1970.

Dodds, Richard. "Where Sex & Spirit Intersect." *Bay Area Reporter,* March 7, 2013: 19. https://issuu.com/bayareareporter/docs/march_14_2013.

Dolan, Jill. *Utopia in Performance: Finding Hope at the Theater.* University of Michigan Press, 2005.

Dolan, Jill. *The Feminist Spectator as Critic.* University of Michigan Press, 1988.

Dyson, Michael Eric. *Know What I Mean? Reflections on Hip-Hop.* Basic Civitas Books, 2007.

Epstein, Rachel. "Butches with Babies: Reconfiguring Gender and Motherhood." *Journal of Lesbian Studies* 6, no. 2 (2002): 41–57.

FORA.tv. "Staceyann Chin and Cynthia Nixon: The Making of MotherStruck." Unfinished Business: The Atlantic LGBT Summit. Posted December 11, 2015. YouTube, https://www.youtube.com/watch?v=ap1PSxk7hUg.

Forbes, Kamilah. *Rhyme Deferred.* In *The Fire This Time: African American Plays for the 21st Century,* edited by Harry J. Elam Jr. and Robert Alexander. Theatre Communications Group, 2004.

Foster, Michèle. "Using Call-and-Response to Facilitate Language Mastery and Literary Acquisition Among African American Studies." *Eric Digest* (July 2002): 1–2.

Gaspin, Jeff. *One on One with John Tesh*—Disc 23. DVD. NBC News, 1991–92.

Gibson, Brian, dir. *The Josephine Baker Story.* DVD. HBO Video, 1991.

Giles, Freda Scott. "Methexis vs. Mimesis: Poetics of Feminist and Womanist Drama." In *Race/Sex,* 175–82. Routledge, 1997.

Goddard, Lynette. *Staging Black Feminisms: Identity, Politics, Performance.* Palgrave-Macmillan, 2007.

González, Anita. "Interview with Sharon Bridgforth." In *solo/black/woman: scripts, interviews, and essays,* edited by E. Patrick Johnson and Ramón H. Rivera Servera, 227–37. Northwestern University Press, 2014.

Grays, Donnetta Lavinia. *the cowboy is dying.* Unpublished manuscript, 2008.

Grays, Donnetta Lavinia. *Last Night and the Night Before.* Samuel French, 2024.

Grays, Donnetta Lavinia. "Make Me Feel Good." Posted 2012. Soundcloud, https://soundcloud.com/donnetta-grays/make-me-feel-good.

Guy-Sheftall, Beverly. *Words of Fire: An Anthology of African-American Feminist Thought.* New Press, 1995.

Halberstam, Jack. "Between Butches." In *butch/femme: Inside Lesbian Gender,* edited by Sally R. Munt, 59–64. Cassell, 1998.

Halberstam, Jack. *Female Masculinity.* Duke University Press, 1998.

Hamilton, Elizabeth Carmel. *Charting the Afrofuturist Imaginary in African American Art: The Black Female Fantastic.* Routledge Press, 2023.

Hammonds, Evelyn. "Black (W)holes and the Geometry of Black Female Sexuality." *differences* 6, nos. 2–3 (1994): 126–45.

Hear Say Diane Neal. "WE'RE GOING TO JAMAICA with Staceyann Chin [FULL EPISODE]." Posted June 30, 2022. YouTube, https://www.youtube.com/watch?v=i2CEcqCF6Zg&t=2693s.

Heath, R. Scott. "Hip_Hop Now: An Introduction." *Callaloo* 29, no. 3 (2006): 714–16. https://www.jstor.org/stable/4488338.

Hill Collins, Patricia. *Black Feminist Thought: Knowledge, Consciousness, and the Politics of Empowerment.* 2nd ed. Routledge, 2009.

Holmes, Shirlene. *A Lady and a Woman* (1990). In *Amazon All Stars: Thirteen Lesbian Plays,* edited by Rosemary Keefe Curb, 186–220. Applause, 1996.

Holmes, Shirlene. "Theatre Rhinoceros Presents *A Lady and a Woman* by Shirlene Holmes." Interview. Posted January 18, 2013. YouTube, https://youtu.be/ozwafHntuac.

hooks, bell. *Feminist Theory: From Margin to Center.* 2nd ed. South End Press, 1984.

hooks, bell. *Talking Back: Thinking Feminist, Thinking Black.* South End Press, 1989.

Hurston, Zora Neale. *Their Eyes Were Watching God* (1937). First Perennial Classics, 1998.

Isherwood, Charles. "Review: In 'MotherStruck!' Staceyann Chin Chronicles Her Quest to Become Pregnant." *New York Times,* December 15, 2015. https://www.nytimes.com/2015/12/15/theater/review-in-motherstruck-staceyann-chin-chronicles-her-quest-to-become-pregnant.html.

Jay-Z. *4:44.* UMG Recordings, 2017.

Johnson, E. Patrick. *Appropriating Blackness: Performance and the Appropriation of Black Authenticity.* Duke University Press, 2003.

Johnson, E. Patrick. *Black. Queer. Southern. Woman: An Oral History.* University of North Carolina Press, 2018.

Johnson, Javon. *Killing Poetry: Blackness and the Making of Slam and Spoken Word Communities.* Rutgers University Press, 2017.

Johnson, Javon. "Manning Up: Race, Gender, and Sexuality in Los Angeles' Slam and Spoken Word Poetry Communities." *Text and Performance Quarterly* 30, no. 4 (2010): 396–419.

Jones, Briona Simone. "Introduction: No Hand, No Gaze." In *Mouths of Rain: An Anthology of Black Lesbian Thought,* edited by Briona Simone Jones, xxv–xxx. New Press, 2021.

Jones, Omi Osun Joni L. *Theatrical Jazz: Performance, Àṣẹ, and the Power of the Present Moment.* The Ohio State University Press, 2015.

Jones, Omi Osun Joni L., Lisa L. Moore, and Sharon Bridgforth, eds. *Experiments in a Jazz Aesthetic: Art, Activism, Academia, and the Austin Project.* University of Texas Press, 2010.

Keegan, Rebecca. "Director Dee Rees on the Importance of Debut 'Pariah' Becoming a Criterion Release: 'We Have to Widen the Canon.'" *Hollywood Reporter,* June 17, 2021. https://www.hollywoodreporter.com/movies/movie-features/dee-rees-pariah-criteron-release-1234967676/.

Keeling, Kara. *The Witch's Flight: The Cinematic, the Black Femme, and the Image of Common Sense.* Duke University Press, 2007.

Keeling, Kara. *Queer Times, Black Futures.* New York University Press, 2019.

Keeling, Kara, Jennifer DeClue, Yvonne Welbon, Jacqueline Stewart, and Roya Rastegar. "*Pariah* and Black Independent Cinema Today: A Roundtable Discussion." *GLQ* 21, nos. 2–3 (June 2015): 423–39.

Kerr, Audrey Elisa. *The Paper Bag Principle.* University of Tennessee Press, 2006.

Köhn, Constanze. "'All Batty Bwoy Haffi Die'—Homophobie in Reggae und Dancehall." *Sexuologie: Zeitschrift für Sexualmedizin, Sexualtherapie und Sexualwissenschaft* 22, no. 1–2 (2015): 61–71. https://doi.org/10.61387/S.2015.12.6.

Kroger, Alicia Kae. "Jazz Form and Jazz Function: An Analysis of *Unfinished Women Cry in No Man's Land While a Bird Dies in a Gilded Cage.*" "Ethnic Theater." Special issue, *MELUS* 16, no. 3 (1989): 99–111.

Lane-Steele, Laura. "Studs and Protest-Hypermasculinity: The Tomboyism Within Black Female Masculinity." *Journal of Lesbian Studies* 15, no. 4 (2011): 480–92.

LeBlanc, Lauren. "Staceyann Chin on Why She Finally Decided to Publish Her Legendary Spoken Word Poetry." *Observer,* October 16, 2019. https://observer.com/2019/10/staceyann-chin-legendary-spoken-word-poet-on-publishing-first-collection-interview/.

Lindeman, Leslie. "Contender—Cinematographer Bradford Young, *Pariah.*" *Below the Line News,* December 14, 2011. https://web.archive.org/web/20141022060450/http://www.btlnews.com/awards/contender-cinematographer-bradford-young-pariah/#.

Lorber, Judith. "Night to His Day: The Social Construction of Gender" (1994). In *Women: Images and Realities—A Multicultural Anthology,* edited by Suzanne Kelly, Gowri Parameswaran, and Nancy Schniedewind, 68–71. 5th ed. McGraw Hill, 2012.

Lorde, Audre. *Sister Outsider: Essays and Speeches* (1984). Crossing Press, 2007.

Millhouse, R. J. *Get Yo' Life: Black Queer Placemaking.* The Ohio State University Press, 2025.

Mims, La Shonda Candace. "Drastic Dyk*s and Accidental Activists: Lesbians, Identity, and The New South." PhD diss., University of Georgia, 2012.

Moore, Darnell L. "Black Radical Love: A Practice." *Public Integrity* 20, no. 4 (2018): 325–28.

Morgan, Betsy Levonian. "A Three Generational Study of Tomboy Behavior." *Sex Roles* 39, nos. 9–10 (1998): 787–800.

Morgan, Joan. "Why We Get Off: Moving Towards a Black Feminist Politics of Pleasure." In *Pleasure Activism: The Politics of Feeling Good,* written and gathered by Adrienne Maree Brown, 32–37. AK Press, 2019.

Morris, Monique W. *Pushout: The Criminalization of Black Girls in Schools.* New Press, 2016.

Morrison, Toni. *Beloved* (1987). First Vintage International ed. Vintage Books, 2004.

Morrison, Toni. *The Bluest Eye* (1970). First Plume Printing. Penguin Books, 1994.

Morrison, Toni. *God Help the Child.* Alfred A. Knopf, 2015.

Morrison, Toni. *Playing in the Dark: Whiteness and the Literary Imagination.* Harvard University Press, 1992.

Morrison, Toni. *Song of Solomon.* Alfred A. Knopf, 1977.

Muñoz, José Esteban. *Cruising Utopia: The Then and There of Queer Futurity.* New York University Press, 2009.

Muñoz, José Esteban. *Disidentifications: Queers of Color and the Performance of Politics.* University of Minnesota Press, 1999.

Musser, Amber Jamilla. "Felt Pleasures: The Jiggle, the Lesbian, and Janelle Monáe's 'Lipstick Lover.'" *Film Quarterly* 77, no. 3 (2024): 44–50. https://doi.org/10.1525/fq.2024.77.3.44.

Nash, Jennifer. *Black Feminism Reimagined: After Intersectionality.* Duke University Press, 2019.

Nash, Jennifer. *Birthing Black Mothers.* Duke University Press, 2021.

Norwood, Kimberly Jade. *Color Matters.* Routledge, 2013.

Nyong'o, Lupita. *Sulwe.* Simon & Schuster, 2019.

Persley, Nicole Hodges. *Sampling and Remixing Blackness in Hip Hop Theater and Performance.* University of Michigan, 2021.

Peterson, Carla L. "Foreword: Eccentric Bodies." In *Recovering the Black Female Body,* edited by Michael Bennett and Vanessa D. Dickerson, ix–xvi. Rutgers University Press, 2001.

Pharr, Suzanne. "Homophobia and Sexism" (1988). In *Women: Images and Realities—A Multicultural Anthology,* edited by Suzanne Kelly, Gowri Parameswaran, and Nancy Schniedewind, 422–25. 5th ed. McGraw-Hill, 2012.

Phelan, Peggy. "The Ontology of Performance: Representation without Reproduction." In *Unmarked: The Politics of Performance,* 146–66. Routledge Press, 1993.

Phillips, Delores. *The Darkest Child,* Soho, 2004.

Porter, Dawn, dir. *Luther: Never Too Much.* Columbia Picture Corporation, 2024.

Ramos, Dino-Ray. "GLAAD Honoree Beyoncé Pays Tribute to 'Godmother' Uncle Jonny on Highly Anticipated 'Renaissance,' Says Album Creates 'A Place Without Judgment.'" GLAAD, July 29, 2022. https://glaad.org/glaad-honoree-beyonce-honors-godm(other-uncle-jonny-renaissance/.

Reddy, Jamila. "The Saints We Call Upon: Staceyann Chin's *MotherStruck!*" *Studio Theatre,* 2016. https://www.studiotheatre.org/plays/play-detail/2016-2017-motherstruck/saints-we-call-upon.

Reed, Allison Rose. *Love and Abolition: The Social Life of Black Queer Performance.* The Ohio State University Press, 2024.

Rees, Dee, dir. *Pariah.* University Studios Home Entertainment, 2011.

Richardson, Matt. *The Queer Limit of Black Memory: Black Lesbian Literature and Irresolution.* The Ohio State University Press, 2013.

Riggs, Marlon T., dir. *Black Is . . . Black Ain't.* California Newsreel, 1995.

Rivera-Servera, Ramón. *Performing Queer Latinidad: Dance, Sexuality, Politics.* University of Michigan Press, 2012.

Rose, Tricia. *The Hip Hop Wars: What We Talk About When We Talk About Hip Hop—and Why It Matters.* Basic Books, 2008.

Royster, Francesca T. "Queering the Jazz Aesthetic: An Interview with Sharon Bridgforth and Omi Osun Joni Jones." *Journal of Popular Music Studies* 25, no. 4 (2013): 537–52.

Russell-Cole, Kathy, Midge Wilson, and Ronald Hall. *The Color Complex.* Anchor Books, 2013.

Sedgwick, Eve Kosofsky. *Epistemology of the Closet.* University of California Press, 1990.

Smith, Marc. "Slam Poetry Movement: Marc Smith at TEDxLUC." Posted May 15, 2013. YouTube, https://www.youtube.com/watch?v=dOpsS9H5dgQ.

Somers-Willett, Susan B. A. *The Cultural Politics of Slam Poetry—Race, Identity, and Performance of Popular Verse in America.* University of Michigan Press, 2009.

Stallings, L. H. Stallings. *A Dirty South Manifesto: Sexual Resistance and Imagination in the New South.* University of California Press, 2019.

Stitt, Jocelyn Fenton. "Disciplining the Unruly (National) Body in Staceyann Chin's *The Other Side of Paradise.*" *Small Axe* 1, vol. 18, no. 3 (45) (2014): 1–17.

Sullivan, Mecca Jamilah. *The Poetics of Difference: Queer Feminist Forms in the African Diaspora.* University of Illinois Press, 2021.

Taylor, Diana. *The Archive and the Repertoire: Performing Cultural Memory in the Americas.* Duke University Press, 2003.

Tift, Kristyl Dawn. "Review of *Performing Queer Latinidad: Dance, Sexuality, Politics* by Ramón H. Rivera-Servera." *Theatre Journal* 66, no. 2 (2014): 311–12.

Townshend, Laurie. *A Mother Apart.* POV/PBS. 2024.

The Trevor Project. "Substance Use and Suicide Risk Among LGBTQ Youth." Posted January 27, 2022. https://www.thetrevorproject.org/research-briefs/substance-use-and-suicide-risk-among-lgbtq-youth-jan-2022/.

Walker, Alice. *In Search of Our Mother's Gardens: Womanist Prose.* Harcourt Brace Jovanovich, 1983.

Wallace, Belinda Deneen, and Tanya L. Shields. "Introduction: Quotidian Futures: Black Queer Subjectivity." *Women, Gender, and Families of Color* 10, no. 2 (2022): 105–17. https://doi.org/10.5406/23260947.10.2.01.

Welbon, Yvonne, and Alexandra Juhasz, eds. *Sisters in the Life: A History of Out Lesbian Media-Making.* Duke University Press, 2018.

White, Patricia. "Pariah (2011): Coming Out in the Middle." In *US Independent Film after 1989: Possible Films,* 133–43. Edinburgh University Press, 2015.

Wilders, JeffriAnne, *Color Stories: Black Women and Colorism in the 21st Century.* Praeger, 2015.

Wilson, James F. *Bulldaggers, Pansies, and Chocolate Babies: Performance, Race, and Sexuality in the Harlem Renaissance.* University of Michigan Press, 2011.

Wonder, Stevie. *Songs in the Key of Life.* Motown Records, 1976.

Woods, Scott. "Poetry Slams: The Ultimate Democracy of Art." *World Literature Today* 82, no. 1 (2008): 16–19.

Woolner, Cookie. *The Famous Lady Lovers: Black Women & Queer Desire Before Stonewall.* University of North Carolina Press, 2023.

Wylam, Lisa Wolford. "The Archive and the Repertoire: Performing Cultural Memory in the Americas." *Theatre Research International* 30, no. 2 (2005): 197–98. https://doi.org/10.1017/S0307883305281415.

Young, Harvey. *Embodying Black Experience: Stillness, Critical Memory, and the Black Body.* University of Michigan Press, 2010.

Zack, Jessica. "'Pariah' a Daring Coming of Age Story: Film Tackles Issues of Sexual Identity." *Times Union*, March 28, 2012. https://www.timesunion.com/entertainment/article/Pariah-a-daring-coming-of-age-story-3441299.php.

INDEX

BLACK PERFORMANCE AND CULTURAL CRITICISM

E. Patrick Johnson, Series Editor
Valerie Lee, Founding Editor Emerita

The Black Performance and Cultural Criticism series includes monographs that draw on interdisciplinary methods to analyze, critique, and theorize Black cultural production. Books in the series take as their object of intellectual inquiry the performances produced on the stage and on the page, stretching the boundaries of both Black performance and literary criticism.

A Conditional Embrace: Black Queer Feminism in Performance
KRISTYL D. TIFT

Get Yo' Life: Black Queer Placemaking
R. J. MILLHOUSE

The Healing Stage: Black Women, Incarceration, and the Art of Transformation
LISA BIGGS

Love and Abolition: The Social Life of Black Queer Performance
ALISON ROSE REED

Black Dragon: Afro Asian Performance and the Martial Arts Imagination
ZACHARY F. PRICE

Staging Black Fugitivity
STACIE SELMON MCCORMICK

Contemporary Black Women Filmmakers and the Art of Resistance
CHRISTINA N. BAKER

Reimagining the Middle Passage: Black Resistance in Literature, Television, and Song
TARA T. GREEN

Conjuring Freedom: Music and Masculinity in the Civil War's "Gospel Army"
JOHARI JABIR

Mama's Gun: Black Maternal Figures and the Politics of Transgression
MARLO D. DAVID

Theatrical Jazz: Performance, Àṣẹ, and the Power of the Present Moment
OMI OSUN JONI L. JONES

When the Devil Knocks: The Congo Tradition and the Politics of Blackness in Twentieth-Century Panama
RENÉE ALEXANDER CRAFT

The Queer Limit of Black Memory: Black Lesbian Literature and Irresolution
MATT RICHARDSON

Fathers, Preachers, Rebels, Men: Black Masculinity in U.S. History and Literature, 1820–1945
EDITED BY TIMOTHY R. BUCKNER AND PETER CASTER

Secrecy, Magic, and the One-Act Plays of Harlem Renaissance Women Writers
TAYLOR HAGOOD

Beyond Lift Every Voice and Sing: The Culture of Uplift, Identity, and Politics in Black Musical Theater
PAULA MARIE SENIORS

Prisons, Race, and Masculinity in Twentieth-Century U.S. Literature and Film
PETER CASTER

Mutha' Is Half a Word: Intersections of Folklore, Vernacular, Myth, and Queerness in Black Female Culture
L. H. STALLINGS

www.ingramcontent.com/pod-product-compliance
Lightning Source LLC
LaVergne TN
LVHW100921110826
845155LV00035B/42

* 9 7 8 0 8 1 4 2 5 9 9 0 0 *